Libertyville

Where Liberty Dwells, There is My Country

By Terry Clothier Thompson

Kansas City Star Books
Kansas City, Missouri

Libertyville

by Terry Clothier Thompson

Edited by Judy Pearlstein

Book design by Kelly Ludwig and Teri Miller

Illustrations by Gary Embry Design/Eric Sears

Photography by Krissy Krauser

Assistant photographer: Rebecca Friend

Production assistance by Jo Ann Groves

Permissions and Loans from:

Leslie Snodgrass – the vintage USA Centennial quilt

Douglas County Historical Society – picture of Civil War soldier and son

Vintage photographs from Terry's collection

Published by Kansas City Star Books

1729 Grand Blvd., Kansas City, Missouri 64108

First edition, first printing

ISBN-13: 978-1-933466-02-6

ISBN-10: 1-933466-02-2

Printed in the United States of America by Walsworth Publishing Co.

To order copies, call StarInfo,

(816-234-4636)

www.PickleDish.com

PickleDish.com

The Quilter's Home Page

★ KANSAS CITY STAR BOOKS

May Bowring, young patriot, age 3, 1887

Table of Contents

Liberty quilt Terry made in 1986 after the 100th birthday
of the installation of the Statue of Liberty

About the Author

Quilt designer and historian Terry Clothier Thompson of Lawrence designed the 2005 block-of-the-month quilt and the other projects in this book. Her Libertyville design is reminiscent of the commemorative quilts seen in the centennial years of America's history, 1876-1900.

The Libertyville quilt – a nod to Philadelphia, birthplace of the Constitution and the site where American independence was declared – is a framed, or center-medallion style. It features a 24-inch square with corner blocks that are bordered by alternating pieced and appliquéd 12-inch blocks The style is easy to assemble and is designed to appeal to both piecers and appliquérs.

Terry has been on the forefront of the current quilt revival. Born into the fifth generation of a Kansas pioneer family, she watched her grandmother and aunt quilt during visits to the family farm called Peace Creek. Her quilting began with the scraps she saved from a dress she made for her daughter, Shannon, in 1967.

In 1973, Thompson opened the Quilting Bee, a store devoted entirely to quilting—an anomaly at the time. The store was originally at 49th Street and State Line Road and later at Seville Square on the Country Club Plaza. It closed in 1984.

A lover of quilt history, Thompson was a principal documenter for the Kansas Quilt Project and a co-author of Kansas Quilts and Quilters, published in 1983 by the University Press of Kansas.

She designs reproduction fabrics for quilts with Barbara Brackman for fabric maker Moda. Thompson also wrote Four Block Quilts: Echoes of History, Pieced Boldly & Appliquéd Freely for The Kansas City Star.

In partnership with her daughter and son-in-law, Shannon and Kent Richards, Terry publishes quilt books and patterns under the label Peace Creek Patterns in Lenexa, Kansas.

Libertyville

"Where Liberty Dwells, There is My Country"
— From vintage fabric

The Civil War ended in 1865 and the work of mending the human spirit of men, women and children began. Women pieced and tied comforters for soldiers on the battlefields and field hospitals, and now a new cause filled their time and put their hands and sewing skills in motion again. Charitable organizations emerged to raise money for widows, orphans, and displaced wounded and recovering soldiers.

The country struggled, both North and South, to regain order, reconstruct the South and help freed slaves find paying jobs to support themselves and their families. For the next ten years, as the people began to heal, women made quilts to commemorate the Civil War, and looked forward to the biggest event about to open in Philadelphia, Pennsylvania, the celebration of the United States of America's 100th birthday. On May 10, 1876 in Fairmont Park, after 10 years of planning and eleven million dollars, with five main buildings on 450 acres, the fair opened with over 30,000 exhibitions. The fair ran for six months and more than 10 million people visited the fair.

The United States showed what a young country could produce in the seven categories on display, mining and metallurgy, manufacturing, science, agriculture, art, machinery and horticulture. Alexander Graham Bell demonstrated the first telephone, and a few states exhibited products from their home region.

The fair influenced citizens to consider moving west for new opportunities for owning their own land. Frederick Diessroth was born in Germany in 1846, and at age 19 sailed to America in the year 1865. He attended the fair and his story is told by Jacob-Sackman,[1] "At the Centennial celebration in Philadelphia, the exhibit of grain, grapes and fruits from the Sunflower State (Kansas) attracted his attention as it did so many others, and as his health was not good, he took a trip to Kansas. After looking over the country, he concluded that Wilson and the surrounding country looked promising. On his return to the city of Brotherly Love, he gathered his German friends about him and made a report. A colony of forty families was organized in April 1877. They came west and landed in Wilson, Kansas." Fabian Hertzman, another German farmer who settled in

Kansas said in a letter sent to his family in the East. "Here in America, there are many wanderers. I like it in Kansas, but if I can get a good price I will sell and move to a better climate. America is Very big, Very big!"[2]

The years following the exhibition brought new ideals to the United States. Patriotism ran high, and the country was relatively at peace for awhile. (In the west, conflict continued between the government and the Indian nations. The Spanish-American war began in 1898.) Attention and money turned to public education, women's rights, and opportunities. Jobs opened for men and women. Leisure time, baseball and horseracing entertained thousands of fans. Railroads crossed the country, uniting families separated by the westward movement.

Women pieced, appliquéd and quilted their quilts on their treadle sewing machines. Because American mills back east produced millions of yards of calico cotton prints, the abundance of fabric allowed the making of thousands of quilts.

Each block for the Libertyville quilt was chosen to commemorate the events of the Centennial years in our United States. "Where Liberty Dwells, There is My Country"

Acknowledgements

With gratitude and appreciation to my friends and colleagues who pieced, appliquéd, quilted, checked the math, and bound the quilts and projects in this book.

Jean Stanclift – Libertyville and Centennial quilts

Pam Mayfield – Technical support and binding Centennial and Libertyville quilts

Karalee Fisher – Crossroads, Jacobs Ladder, Churn Dash baby quilt

Lori Kukuk – quilted Libertyville and USA Centennial

Rosie Mayhew – quilted Temperance crib quilt

Maggie Bonanami – Liberty Bell pincushion

Susie Kepley – Miss Libby punch needle

Ilyse Moore – copy editing

The Mahaffie Farmstead Staff: Tim Talbot, DeWayne Hill, and Geoff Bahr with Dan, (the beautiful palomino) and special thanks to Alexis Radil.

Photographers – Krissy Krauser and Rebecca Friend

[1] Kansas State Historical Society, [2] IBID

Making the Libertyville Quilt

BEFORE YOU BEGIN:

Make sure you read through all directions before you begin the quilt or projects.

FABRIC REQUIREMENTS

BACKGROUND

❧ 12 different fat quarters of white shirtings for background of blocks. You may choose any neutral background that contrasts with the other colors in the blocks.
(The total yardage is ❧ 3 yards for the blocks and ❧ 1 yard for the center square.)

ADDITIONAL FABRICS FOR BLOCKS

❧ 3 fat quarters of each color: indigo (navy blue), bright blue, red or cinnamon red (madder), turkey red (a brighter red), soft browns or red prints on a black background. (Use stripes, small and medium florals, shaded fabrics and white shirtings.)
❧ Select a variety of scraps for flowers, such as yellow or gold prints, sweet pinks for both the center square and blocks.
❧ Buy 1 fat quarter each of a light, medium and dark green for vines, stems and leaves.

SETTING TRIANGLES

❧ 3 1/2 yards of blue or a color that contrasts with the block backgrounds. Buy 5/8 yard of a contrasting print for the 4 triangles around the center square.

FOR THE BORDERS

❧ Borders are 12" wide and require 3 yards of a white shirting or the same neutral in the background of the blocks.

TIP:

Thanks to Lise Russ for this great idea.

Here's a wonderful tip that helps you use this book as you make your templates and patterns.

1. Buy a 3-ring notebook with a plastic insert on the front and back cover.

2. Take your book to a printing company and ask them to remove the spine of the book. Take your notebook with you.

3. Have them punch 3 holes in the pages so that they will fit into your binder.

4. Place the front cover of the book into the plastic front cover of the notebook, and place back cover of book into the back insert of the notebook.

5. Place the entire copy of your book into the inside of the notebook.

Now you have easy access to each page, you may remove any page to line up templates that require taping together. It is so easy to draw the appliqués on a flat surface rather than trying to trace into the fold of the book. It's a great idea for any book with appliqué templates.

Libertyville
92" x 92"
Stitched by Jean Stanclift
Quilted by Lori Kukuk
McClouth, Kansas

Centennial Block

12" finished square

Stitched by Jean Stanclift, Lawrence, Kansas

The first block in the sampler is the Centennial Commemorative block. American cotton mills in the East produced inexpensive floral prints, stripes, shirtings, and conversation prints. Out of an abundance of dress-weight cotton fabric came an abundance of pieced and appliquéd quilts. During the centennial years women wore dresses made of madder red (cinnamon, barn red, terra cotta), brilliant blues, bright pink calicoes, and soft browns. Terry's quilt reflects these period colors.

Commemorative prints designed to celebrate America's 100th birthday appeared in quilts along with quilt patterns that made a social comment from women who had not yet voted in an election.

The history of the centennial years in America, 1876-1900, is a celebration of the golden age of education, the arts, new opportunities for men and women, and the ideals and leisure time never before experienced by middle class Americans. The patterns chosen for this sampler quilt relate to the patriotism celebrated at the Centennial Exposition in Philadelphia, Pennsylvania in 1876.

FABRIC

❦ Small print shirting or any neutral for the background. Shirtings range from white to a creamy tan background. The figures are small florals, geometrics, stripes or conversation prints. I chose a white background to reproduce the original look of white or slightly off-white shirtings of 1876-1900. Antique "whites" from that period have yellowed a bit, so choose whatever background you like. All future blocks will have a different shirting as a background.

❦ Blue and red, or a madder red, which is a cinnamon red. Stripes and small prints work well in this block.

Tip: Contrasting colors work best in all blocks.

ROTARY CUTTING THE FABRIC

❦ **PIECE A:** Cut 4 white 3 1/2" squares.

❦ **PIECE B:** (Background) Cut 1 white 7 1/4" square. Cut this square from corner to corner on both diagonals to create 4 triangles.

❦ **PIECE C:** (Red Star points) Cut 2 - 4 1/4" red squares. Cut each square from corner to corner on both diagonal lines to create 8 triangles.

❦ **PIECE D:** (Blue rectangle) Cut 4 - 2 5/8" x 4 3/4" rectangles.

❦ **PIECE E:** (Red center square) Cut one 4 3/4" square.

STITCHING THE FABRIC

❦ Follow the piecing diagram to easily set the Centennial block. There is no "setting in" corners, just straight seam sewing.

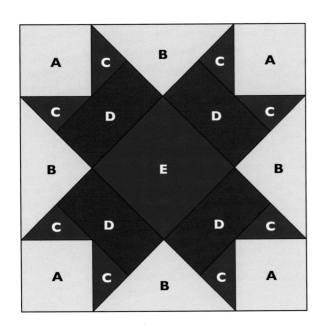

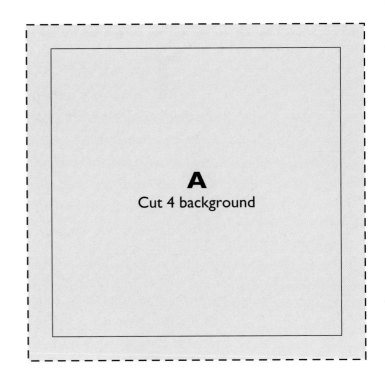

A
Cut 4 background

C
Cut 8 red

B
Cut 4 background

E
Cut 1 red

D
Cut 4 blue

Centennial Block Pillow

FABRIC REQUIREMENTS

🐚 1/2 yard of a small print shirting or any neutral for the background, backing and binding.

🐚 1 fat quarter of a blue and red, or a madder red, which is a cinnamon red. Stripes and small prints work well in this pattern. Contrasting colors work best in all blocks.

🐚 1/2 yard for back of pillow and binding

🐚 2 printed border fabrics for side borders 2 1/2" x 12 1/2"

🐚 12" x 16" pillow form

CUTTING DIRECTIONS

🐚 Follow directions for cutting Centennial block

🐚 For the two side borders, cut 2 strips, 2 1/2" x 12 1/2"

🐚 For backing, cut 2 pieces 11" x 12 1/2"

🐚 Cut 2" wide, straight grain strips for binding.

SEWING DIRECTIONS

🐚 Piece the Centennial Block.

🐚 Sew border print to each side of the block.

🐚 Turn under 1" hem on 2 sides of pillow backing for the opening.

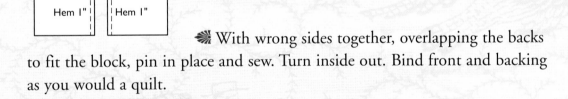

🐚 With wrong sides together, overlapping the backs to fit the block, pin in place and sew. Turn inside out. Bind front and backing as you would a quilt.

🐚 For quilters piping, follow the directions in the WCTU pillow directions on page 70.

🐚 Place pillow form inside pillow.

"Centennial" Block Pillow on right

12" x 16"

Stitched by Karalee Fisher, Perry, Kansas

Liberty Bell

"Liberty Bell"
12" finished square
Stitched by Jean Stanclift

Colonial America relied on the town bell to notify citizens of impending dangerous storms, enemy raids and death tolls for funerals. The ringing of the bell woke everyone each morning and each night for the evening curfew, and it was a call to assembly of town leaders.

In Philadelphia, in 1751, Isaac Norris, Speaker of the Assembly, placed an order for a "Bell from England to be purchased for their use we take the Liberty to apply ourselves to thee to get us a good Bell of about two thousand pounds weight." Norris asked, "Let the Bell be cast by the best workmen and examined carefully before it is shipped with the following words well shaped in large letters round it, 'By order of the Assembly of the Province of Pensylvania for the Statehouse in the city of Philadelphia, 1752', and underneath, 'Proclaim Liberty thro all the Land to all Inhabitants Thereof - Levitt. XXVIO'". (Norris misspelled Pennsylvania on his order and therefore Pennsylvania was spelled with one "N" on the bell.)

Whitechappel Bell Foundry received the order and within ten months shipped the bell to America. On September 1, 1752 Norris sent word to his assistant, "The bell is come ashore and in good order and tho we have not yet tryd the sound."

The Great Bell was temporarily hung on a low frame and someone flung the clapper from one side of the bell to the other causing "a loud bong followed by a discordant hum and quiver." - Charles Michael Boland, "Ring in the Jubilee"

Immediately a crack appeared ruining the bell. The bell was broken apart and the metal recast in an American foundry twice before the final bell, now known as the Liberty Bell, was achieved. In 1841 the bell cracked again after 100 years of service and is now retired.

This American symbol of freedom was rung at the first public reading of the Declaration of Independence on July 8, 1776. "Today the image of the Liberty Bell reminds us of the struggle of few for the freedom of a nation. -Boland, "Ring in the Jubilee"

FABRIC

- Brown for bell, clapper, and handle
- Green for acorn caps and leaves
- Scrap of red or rusty red for acorns
- Neutral or shirting for a 12 1/2" background block.

DIRECTIONS

◉ Using a shirting or neutral fabric cut a 12 1/2" square (this includes seam allowance) for the background block.

◉ Add a 1/4" seam allowance to all appliqué templates. Prepare patterns for hand or machine appliqué.

◉ Being careful not to stretch, place the background block on point. Fold the square in half from corner to corner. Lightly and gently press the fold for a guideline. This is a bias line, so do not iron, just press a soft line.

◉ Using the guideline and picture, arrange all appliqué pieces. Place the bell, piece A, first.

◉ The bell handle pattern piece B, is also the clapper pattern. Just turn it upside down. Place the handle and the clapper, tucking the ends under the bell.

◉ Arrange the leaves piece C, to fit a circle around the bell. Tuck each stem under the top of the leaf below it.

◉ Place the acorns and acorn caps, pieces D and E.

◉ Pin and baste all appliqué pieces. (Appliqué in your favorite manner or refer to Terry's KC Star book, Four Block Quilts, Pieced Boldly and Appliquéd Freely, for her easy methods of Appliqué.) Sew with the running or blind stitch.

◉ Embroider a crack in the bell.

Centennial Woven Coverlet owned by Barbara Brackman

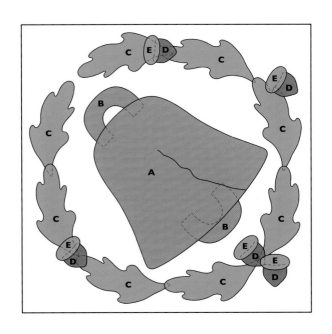

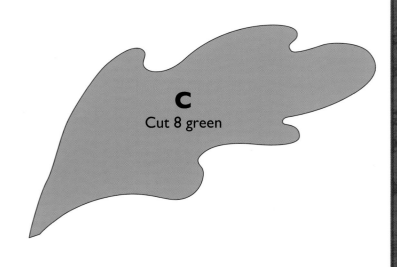

C
Cut 8 green

(For clapper, place bottom of bell on this line.)

B
Cut 2 brown

E
Cut 5 green

D
Cut 5 red

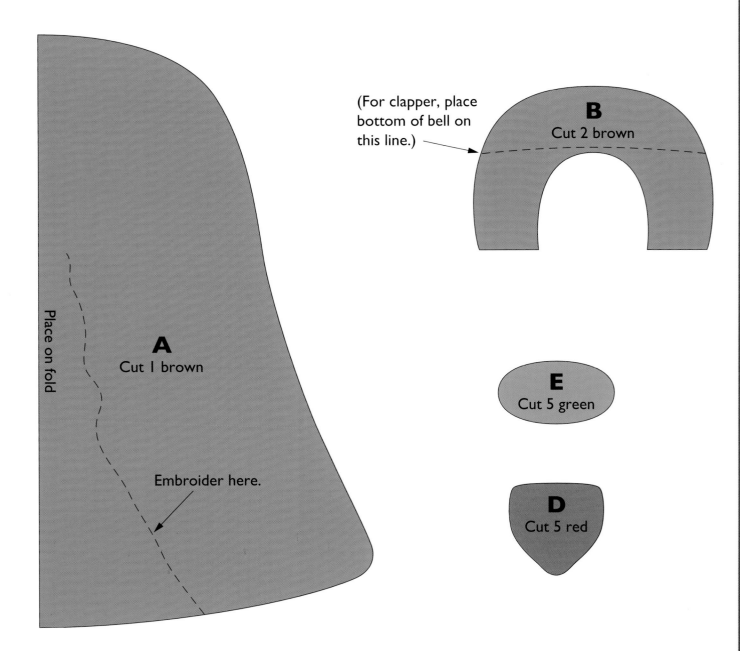

Place on fold

A
Cut 1 brown

Embroider here.

Liberty Bell Pincushion

FABRIC REQUIREMENTS

* 12" x 18" tan velvet (Maggie overdyed Rit's pearl gray on tan velvet.)
* 7" x 8 1/2" off-white wool
* Scraps of blue and red wool
* Cotton, wool roving or poly stuffing
* Thin cardboard
* 1 medium button
* Patriotic ribbon (14" red, white, blue)
* Matching thread

CUTTING AND SEWING DIRECTIONS

I use freezer paper to trace the pattern on the dull side. Press patterns to the wrong side of velvet. Cut out with a 1/4" seam allowance added as you cut.

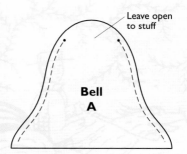

Leave open to stuff

Bell
A

STEP 1

* Stitch bell (A) right sides together down each side from stitching between the dots. See figure 1. Stop sewing 1/4" from bottom of bell.

STEP 2

* Cut 1 velvet piece B.
* Cut 1 cardboard shape for Piece B using the dotted line for the pattern. the cardboard will stabilize the bottom of the bell to help it stand.
* Cut a piece of cotton batting the same size as cardboard. Clip around the bottom (B).
* Stack bell bottom, batting, then cardboard.

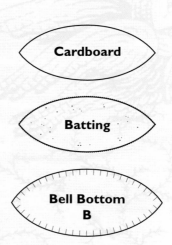

Cardboard

Batting

Bell Bottom
B

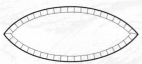

* Fold the clipped edges over and glue down with a glue stick.

STEP 3

❦ Stuff bell with your choice of stuffing.

❦ Turn under 1/4" seam allowance on the bell. Stitch the bell (A) to bell bottom (B). Whipstitch all around bottom.

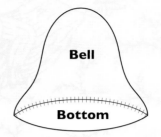

STEP 4

❦ For band around the bell, cut a velvet strip 1" x 18".

❦ Turning over the 1/4" seam allowance as you sew, whipstitch the band around the bottom of bell, over the seam attaching the bell to the bell bottom. Ease in edge if needed.

STEP 5

❦ Cut out Liberty letters and star for the back of the bell. Appliqué with a simple whipstitch.

STEP 6

❦ Make the loop for the top of the bell. Cut a 1" x 5" strip of velvet and roll it with your fingers to form a loop. Whipstitch raw edge and fold into a loop. Tack to the top of the bell, tucking raw edges inside the bell.

❦ Tie ribbon around loop.

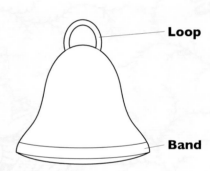

STEP 7 - NEEDLECASE

❦ Whipstitch 2 wool pieces together (piece C), and add the blue field (canton), 3 red stripes and star. Refer to picture.

❦ Make a buttonhole on the stripe end. Use a buttonhole stitch. Stitch the small white oval to the bell bottom to hold needles. Tack the needlecase on the blue field end to the bell bottom. Add button for closure.

Front

Back

Bottom

"Liberty Bell"

Designed and created for Libertyville by Maggie Bonanami, Lexington, Missouri

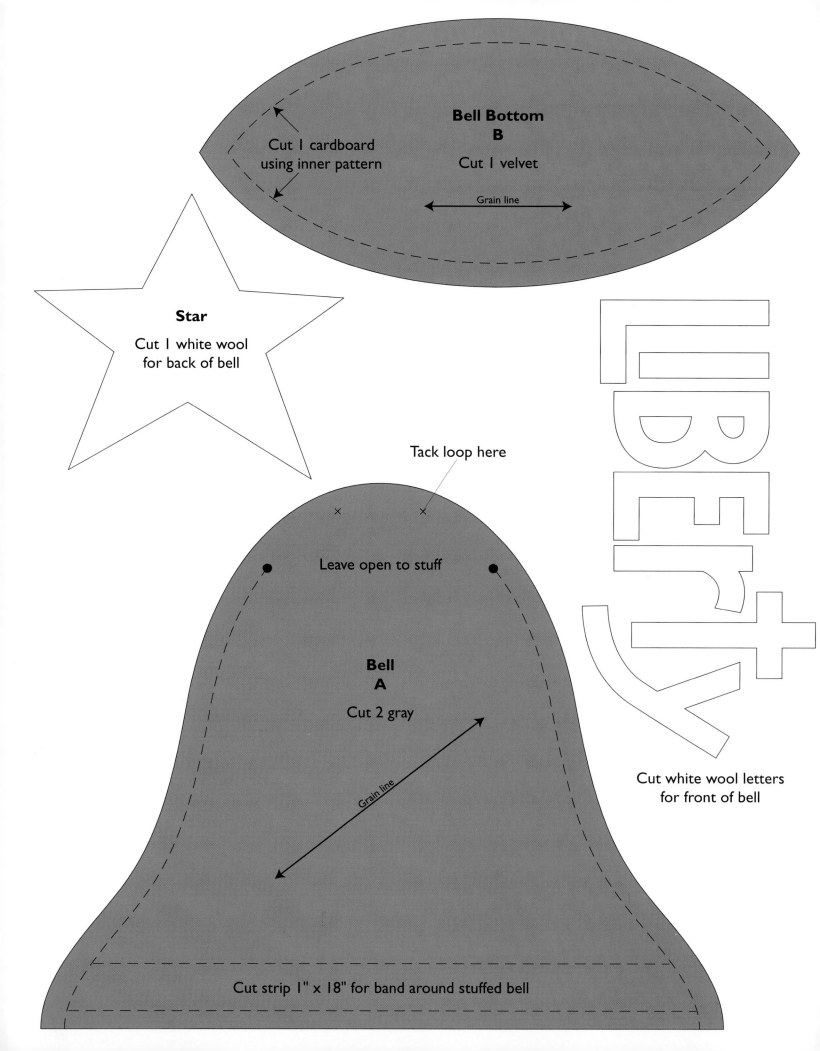

Bell Bottom
B

Cut 1 velvet

Cut 1 cardboard
using inner pattern

Grain line

Star

Cut 1 white wool
for back of bell

LiBErty

Tack loop here

Leave open to stuff

Bell
A

Cut 2 gray

Grain line

Cut white wool letters
for front of bell

Cut strip 1" x 18" for band around stuffed bell

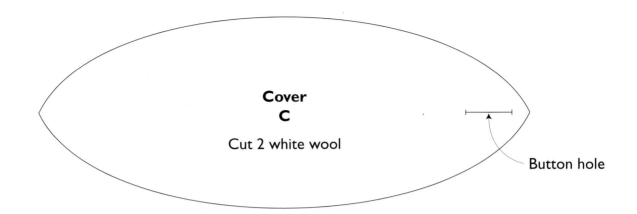

**Cover
C**

Cut 2 white wool

Button hole

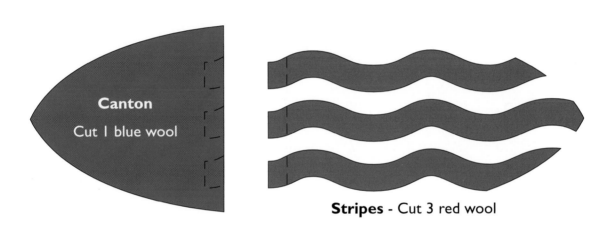

Canton

Cut 1 blue wool

Stripes - Cut 3 red wool

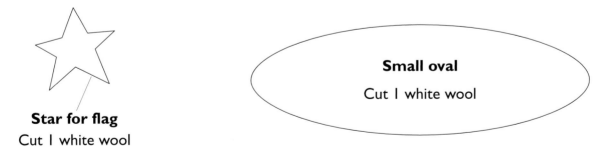

Star for flag

Cut 1 white wool

Small oval

Cut 1 white wool

Sherman's March

"Sherman's March"

12" square

Stitched by Jean Stanclift

Quilt pattern names often change after a major historical event takes place. At the end of the Civil War many patterns became known as Union Star for northern quilt makers celebrating Union victories. The Sherman's March pattern had several names and is better known to contemporary quilters as Churn Dash, Monkey Wrench or Hole in the Barn Door. Commemorative patterns such as Lincoln's Platform and Sherman's March suggest a northern and southern source for the commemorative pattern name. Sherman's March commemorates the famous "March to the Sea" through the Confederate states by Sherman's Union troops looting and burning farms and cities and striking terror into the hearts of unprotected southern women.

FABRIC

🌺 Red

🌺 Neutral, either white or off-white shirting for background

ROTARY CUTTING DIRECTIONS

PIECE A: Cut 2-4 7/8" squares of red and 2-4 7/8" squares of neutral fabric. Cut squares from corner to corner on both diagonals to give you 4 neutral and 4 red triangles.

PIECE B: Cut 4 red and 4 neutral 2 1/2" x 4 1/2" rectangles.

PIECE C: Cut 1 neutral 4 1/2" square.

SEWING DIRECTIONS

🌺 Following the diagram, sew neutral and red triangles, piece A for corners.

🌺 Sew neutral and red rectangles, piece B.

🌺 Set in three rows as you would a nine-patch square.

🌺 Press seams to one side.

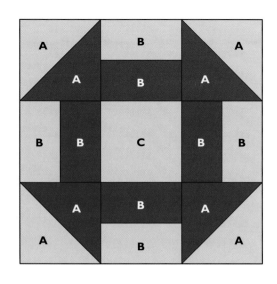

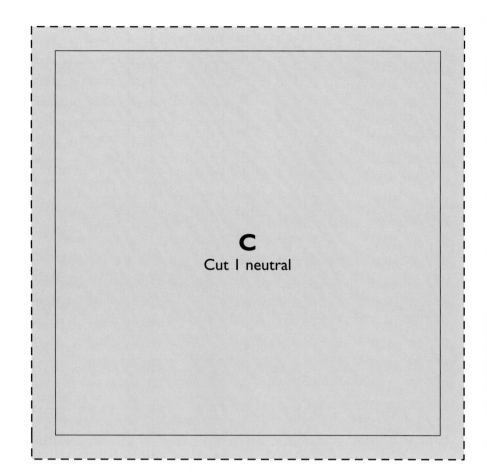

C
Cut 1 neutral

Piecing the block

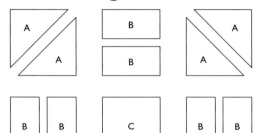

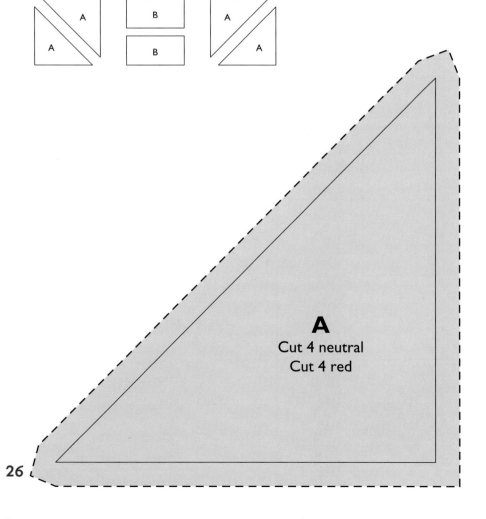

A
Cut 4 neutral
Cut 4 red

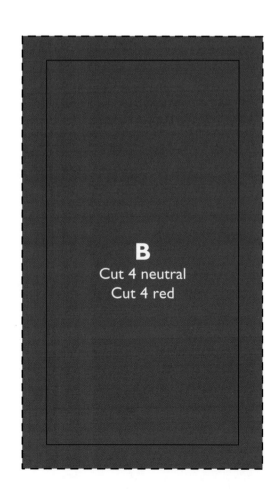

B
Cut 4 neutral
Cut 4 red

Churn Dash Baby Quilt and Triangle Pillow
36" x 36"
Stitched by Karalee Fisher • Perry, Kansas

Churn Dash Baby Quilt and Triangle Pillow

QUILT YARDAGE

❈ Fat quarters of a good variety of pink, blue, red, brown, green and light cream fabrics. Choose large, medium and small prints for variety and interest. Contrast the colors as you plan your blocks.

DIRECTIONS FOR QUILT:

❈ Follow directions for the Sherman's March 12 1/2" block.
❈ Set 9 blocks in 3 rows of 3 blocks.

PRAIRIE POINTS FOR BORDER:

❈ Cut 56 - 3" squares out of your scraps.
❈ Fold the squares on the diagonal and press, fold again and press.
❈ Fold the left corner over to the right corner and press.

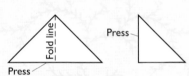

❈ Place the raw edge of the pressed squares (now triangles) on raw edge of the quilt top, starting at corners of quilt.
❈ Fit the rest of the triangles down the sides and bottom of the quilt top, fitting the corners into the fold of the one next to it. You can fudge the points in the middle of the quilt if needed.

❈ Adjust the prairie points and pin in place when you are satisfied with the placement.
❈ Turn the points over and check to see if all raw edges are even with the raw edge of the quilt, and the corners overlap into the next point. Adjust the position of points if needed.
❈ Using a 1/4" machine basting stitch, sew all around the quilt, catching the quilt top and prairie points. (See figure #2 above.)
❈ Cut batting 1" larger than the top.

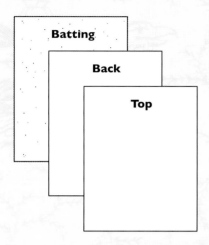

❋ Layer the batt, then the back, right side up, then the top right side down.

❋ Stitch on the basting line, catching the batt, the back, and top all at the same time. Leave an opening for turning, and hand stitch the opening closed.

❋ To quilt, stitch by machine in the ditch between blocks and around the square of each block.

(Easy - There is no binding.)

TRIANGLE PILLOW

❋ Make a 12 1/2" Churn Dash block. Baste a 12 1/2" square of batt to the block, trim away extra batt. The batt gives body to the block.

❋ Make 10 prairie points out of your scraps.

❋ Fit 5 points as seen in figure 2, on just two edges of the block. Fit the right and left points 1/8" from edge, last.

❋ Baste around 2 edges with the points, to secure them.

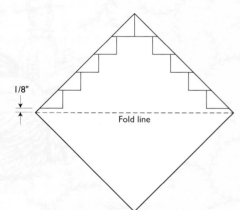

❋ Fold the block with the right sides together, stitch a 1/4" seam allowance, leaving an opening for turning the right side out.

❋ Turn, stuff and stitch the opening closed by hand.

Tulip Wheel

"*Tulip Wheel*"
12" square
Stitched by Jean Stanclift

*T*he Centennial Exposition of 1876 was in Philadelphia, Pennsylvania, known as the City of Brotherly Love. Pennsylvania is famous for the state's rich heritage of quilts. Quiltmakers of Pennsylvania German descent sewed boldly, appliquéing and piecing calicos of bright reds, yellows, pinks, double blues, and spring greens. Favorite patterns included tulips, roses, "Star of Bethlehem," "Love Apple," "Le Moyne Star" and "Nine Patch."

The "Tulip Wheel" pattern shown here is a more unusual pattern drawn from an old block that Terry purchased on a trip to Pennsylvania. The colors are typical of the area.

Remember to set all blocks on point when it is time to set the Libertyville quilt together.

FABRIC

- ✺ Shirting or neutral for a 12 1/2" square for the background block.
- ✺ Indigo blue (navy blue) for the 4 tulips and 4 stems
- ✺ Yellow or gold for centers of tulips, and the 1-inch center square in the middle of the stems.
- ✺ 1 - 8" square of red for the center circle

DIRECTIONS

- ✺ Cut a 12 1/2" square for the background. This includes the 1/4" seam allowance.
- ✺ Prepare all patterns for hand or machine appliqué.
- ✺ Prepare background block with pressed guidelines. Fold the background square in half from corner to corner on the diagonal. Gently finger-press the fold. Repeat on the other opposing corners. The fold lines make an X and a center point as a guide for placing the red circle and the flower stems. Fold circle in half, finger press, fold again, finger press to find the center of the circle.
- ✺ Lay out the red circle, piece C, in center of the square. Pin in place.
- ✺ Place the two stems, piece D on pressed lines.

✺ Cut out four tulips, piece A, and four centers, piece B. Appliqué the center to the tulip.

✺ Place a tulip at the end of each of the stems pointing towards the corners. Tuck the ends of stems under the tulips.

✺ Place the gold square, piece E, in the center of the block where the stems cross.

✺ Baste all in place. Appliqué.

(Tips for hand appliqué: Make templates by drawing around the appliqué patterns on a sheet of plastic template. Place template on the right side of the fabric and draw around the template. Cut 1/4" seam allowance from the pencil line. This pencil line is your guide for turning under the 1/4" seam allowance as you appliqué.)

Note: The tulip templates are used again in the center medallion block and in the Tulip Wheel penny mat shown below.

"Tulip Wheel" Penny Rug

18 1/2" circle

Stitched by Terry Thompson

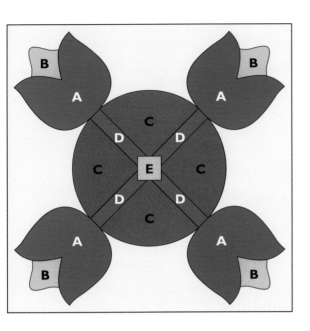

E
Cut 1 gold

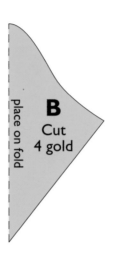

place on fold

B
Cut
4 gold

D Cut 2 blue

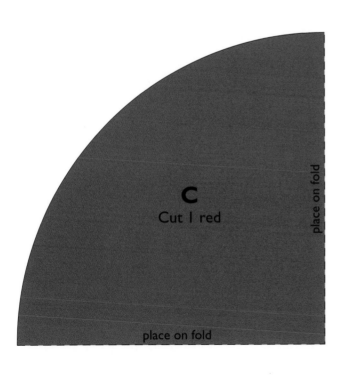

C
Cut 1 red

place on fold

place on fold

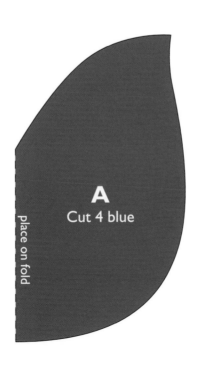

place on fold

A
Cut 4 blue

Tulip Wheel Wool Penny Rug

Use the Tulip Wheel pattern.

YARDAGE

- 15" x 15" square of black wool for the large center circle. The circle pattern is 14 1/2". Cut out circle from freezer paper. Press onto black fabric, cut around the circle.
  - 1/4 yard of blue-green wool for center 7 1/2" circle
  - 1/8 yard for 2 - 1/2" x 6 1/2" stems of spring green wool
  - 1/8 yard of red for 1 - 1" center square and 4 tulips
  - 1/8 yard of gold for centers of 4 tulips

CUTTING

- Use the tulip wheel pattern.
- Use all colors to cut 15 half-circles for outside border; alternate red, gold, and green.

SEWING DIRECTIONS

- Lay out center circle, stems, square, and tulips. Pin and baste.
- Sew around all raw edges with the buttonhole stitch with matching colors of #8 perle cotton thread.
- Lay out 1/2 circles around the black circle, slightly overlapping each end with the next half circle. Pin and baste in place.
- With black thread, stitch the half circles to the black circle with a running stitch in black perle cotton thread.

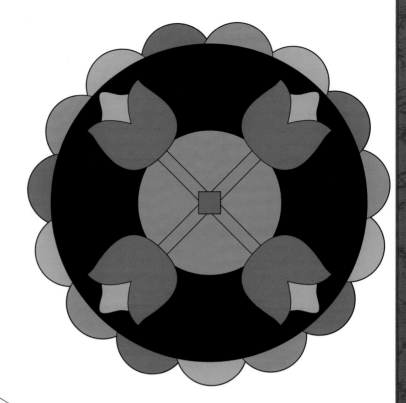

Border Half Circle

Cut 5 red
Cut 5 gold
Cut 5 blue green

Place on fold

Large Circle

Cut 1 black

Place on fold

Center Circle

Cut 1 blue green

Place on fold

Place on fold

Crossroads

"Crossroads"
12" square
Stitched by Jean Stanclift

In 1862, the Homestead Act changed the lives of men and women living in the eastern United States. For $10 one could settle in the Plains states on 160 acres of government land. If you built a claim shack and worked the land for five years, the land was deeded over to you.

Thousands of young men and women left their crowded homes and moved west. Every mode of transportation was used: wagons, trains, horseback, riverboats. Some folks made the trip on foot.

Farming the land or running a cattle or sheep ranch appealed to these young Americans. Thousands of people attending the Centennial Exposition in 1876 in Philadelphia saw exhibits of new technology and displays of farm produce from the Plains states. They were inspired to make their dreams of owning land come true. Homes were built and farms flourished as the railroads moved their produce and cattle to Chicago and the eastern states.

The "Crossroads" block represents the abundance of choices available to Americans. Do we go to California and mine for gold, go as far as Kansas and raise wheat or cattle, go to Oklahoma for the "land rush" and stake a claim, or possibly start a school in a sod house in the middle of a Nebraska prairie?

FABRIC

❧ Blue for pieces C, E and 4 of D

❧ Neutral, either white or off-white shirting, for pieces A and B, and 8 of D.

Group at Ottawa Kans. 1876

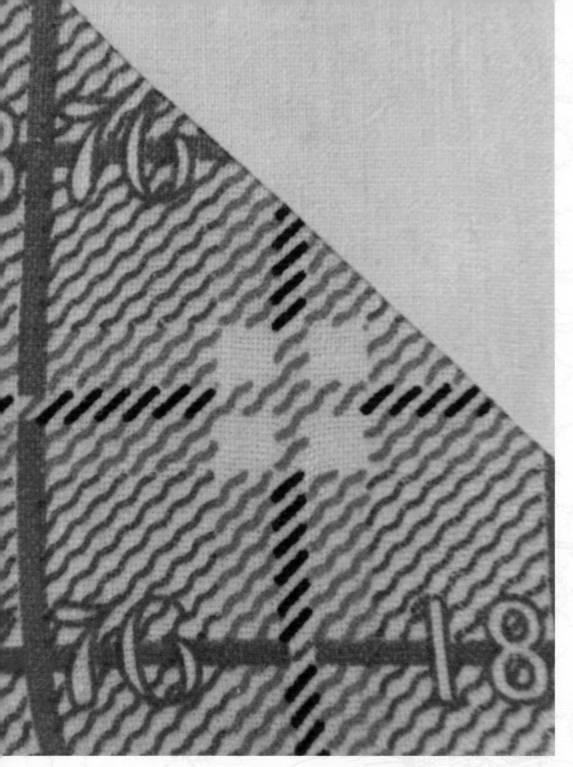

CUTTING DIRECTIONS

❦ Piece A: Cut 4 white pieces from template A.

❦ Piece B: Cut 8 white pieces from template B.

❦ Piece C: Cut 4 - 2 1/2" blue squares. Cut squares from corner to corner on the diagonals to give you 4 triangles per square or a total of 16 blue triangles.

❦ Piece D: Cut 8 white and 4 blue 1 7/8" x 4 1/2" rectangles.

❦ Piece E: Cut 1 blue 4 1/2" square.

SEWING DIRECTIONS

❦ Sew pieces together referring to piecing diagram.

❦ Assemble block as you would a nine-patch block. Refer to diagram for placement.

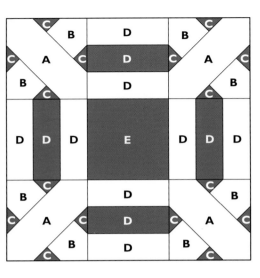

Piecing the block

C
Cut 16
blue

D
Cut 8 white
Cut 4 blue

B
Cut 8 white

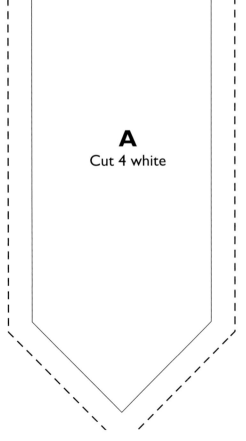

A
Cut 4 white

E
Cut 1 blue

Crossroads Table or Pillow Cover

"Crossroads"
Table or
Pillow Cover
24" x 36"
Pieced and quilted by
Karalee Fisher

FABRIC REQUIREMENTS FOR SIX BLOCKS

- 1/2 yard of 2 different black prints
- 1 fat quarter each of 2 different reds
- 1 fat quarter each of 2 different white shirtings
- 1 yard for backing and binding

CUTTING DIRECTIONS

USE TEMPLATES FOR:

- Piece A: Cut 24 red pieces.
- Piece C: Cut 96 black pieces.
- Piece D: Cut 24 white, 24 red, and 24 black 1 7/8" by 4 1/2" rectangles.
- Piece E: Cut 6 black 4 1/2" squares.

ROTARY CUT:

- Piece B: Cut 12 - 2 1/2" white squares. Cut in half on diagonal, then cut on diagonal again to get 48 pieces from template B.

SEWING DIRECTIONS

- Sew pieces together referring to piecing diagram.
- Set six blocks into 2 rows.
- Quilt in the ditch (along seam lines). Avoid fancy quilting as that would distract from the visual effect of the blocks chaining from one to another.

TIPS: Karalee placed double-sided tape on back of template A. Place ruler next to template and rotary cut around the template. No plastic template necessary. Also, press every other block's seams in the opposite direction when sewing blocks into rows.

Set Sail for America,

"Set Sail for America"
12"square
Stitched by Jean Stanclift

Land of Dreams

European immigrants began populating the eastern shores of America as early as 1624. Early settlers included the Dutch, French and English. By 1775, German Palatines, Swedish, Scandinavian and Irish immigrants started new colonies, bringing with them their traditions, trade skills and work ethics.

Between 1750 and 1850 the population of Europe doubled, so peasants and tradesmen looked to America as a new source of food and work. The dream of owning one's own land and enjoying the freedom of religion, inspired husbands and fathers to leave their wives and children in their native country and come to America for a better life. When jobs were found, money was sent to their families who paid $30.00 fare to board the ships sailing from European docks to America, the Land of Dreams.

The voyage took ten to sixteen days to cross the Atlantic, but to the people packed into the bottom of the ship, called steerage, it seemed an endless ordeal. Plagued with no fresh air, seasickness, poor food and little chance of good hygiene or sanitary conditions, everyone but the upper class passengers suffered greatly. Space limited families to one or two trunks or bags. Many women and children wore all of their clothes, layer upon layer. Wives and young girls sewed their only money and jewels into the hems of their skirts for

safekeeping. There are stories of children as young as 10 or 12 years old that had been sent alone on the ship to be met by friends or a relative on the New York docks where ships from every country unloaded their weary passengers. Between 1850-1890 immigrants were taken to Castle Garden, a port of entry that more than 8-million people passed through. Another processing station was an island called Gull Island, which the native Indians used for oyster fishing. A later owner of the island was Samuel Ellis, whose descendents later sold it to New York City.

Steamships called Victoria, Kaiser Wilhelm, and Vincenzo Florio docked at piers along the Hudson River in New York. From there, immigrants took ferries over to Ellis Island where they waited in long lines to be examined for physical or mental illness. Anyone with eye diseases, tuberculosis, heart or breathing problems could not stay in the U.S. and was sent back to Europe. After the Civil War, about 26 million people came to America.

"1892"

FABRIC

- Shirting or neutral for the background block
- 6" x 11" of a brown/black print for ship
- Blue for the 3 sails
- Scrap of brown stripe for the 2 masts
- Scrap of red for flag
- Gold or yellow perle cotton for "America" embroidered on flag

DIRECTIONS

- Cut a 12 1/2" square for the block background.
- Cut out the sails, masts, ship and flag (Embroider "America" on flag before appliquéing).
- Fold the block in half from corner to corner on the diagonal, and gently finger-press in a line. This is a guideline for placing the ship, masts, sails and flag.
- Place the bottom of the ship 3 1/4" from the bottom corner. Arrange the short and tall masts and the sails. Refer to picture for placement. The flag rests on the tall mast about 3" from the top corner of the block.

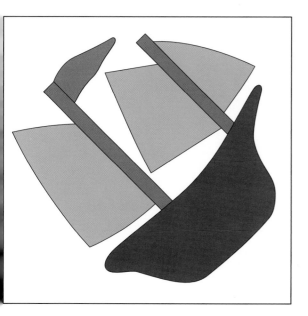

Ship
Cut 1 black/brown print

**#1
Front Sail**
Cut 1 blue

AMERICA

Flag
Cut 1 red

45

Tall Mast
Cut 1 brown stripe

**#2
Middle Sail**
Cut 1 blue

**#3
Back Sail**
Cut 1 blue

Short Mast
Cut 1 brown stripe

Ship in a bottle
18 1/2" x 31 1/2"

"Ship in a Bottle"
18" x 32"
Sewn by Terry Thompson

This project may be worked in cotton or wool, made into a table or floor rug, or may be made to hang on the wall framed or unframed. My ship is made of wool.

FABRIC REQUIREMENTS

- 1 yard light brown for background
- 24" of a bottle green/blue for the bottle
- 5" x 11" wool tweed in medium brown for ship
- 7" x 11" dyed wool in tan splotched with medium brown for 3 sails
- 3" x 7" dark brown wool for masts and window
- 3 1/2" x 4" dark red wool splotched with black for anchor
- 2" x 6 1/2" gold wool for America banner
- 2" x 4" lighter red for 1876 flag
- 12" x 41" medium blue wool for water under ship and the wave borders
- 2" x 3" light greenish blue for cork

TIPS

I used a #8 DMC perle cotton thread for the buttonhole stitch around each appliqué. The colors I used were light blue, green, rusty brown, black, yellow, red, and an embroidery needle with an eye that will take perle cotton #8.

You can match your thread colors or contrast them, although variegated thread did not work well for me on this project. It looked too modern and I was going for an old 19th century look.

The great thing about appliquéing with wool is you don't have to turn over the edges, it won't ravel, and the colors are so vivid.

CUTTING DIRECTIONS

❨ Use ship templates from Set Sail for America block. To reverse the direction of the ship for this pattern, reverse templates of the ship and sails. Use the dull side of freezer paper to trace patterns, not the shiny side.

❨ Cut out each pattern and press onto the chosen wool.

❨ Tape the bottle pattern together in 3 pieces along the dotted lines.

SEWING DIRECTIONS

❨ Place the bottle in the middle of the background. Referring to the picture, place and pin all pattern pieces, basting everything but the wave borders.

❨ Sew all pattern pieces with perle cotton in the buttonhole stitch. Use the long stitch over the windows and a long whipstitch over the masts.

❨ Chain stitch a line from the anchor to the ship.

❨ Sew the blue water at the bottom of the ship.

❨ Embroider the words "America" on the banner and "1876" in the flag.

❨ Borders: Cut 2 wave borders for the top and the bottom of the background, 32" long. Cut 2 side borders 19" long.

I cut a long piece of felt the same size as the rug for support and to give the piece body. Sew a sleeve on the back and hang.

Chain stitch
black floss

Anchor
Cut 1 red

Flag
Cut 1 red

Banner
Cut 1 gold - red floss

Ship windows
Cut 4 brown

Blue Wave Border

Cut 2 strips 19" - blue
Cut 2 strips 32 1/2" - blue

Water at bottom of ship

Cut 1 blue

50

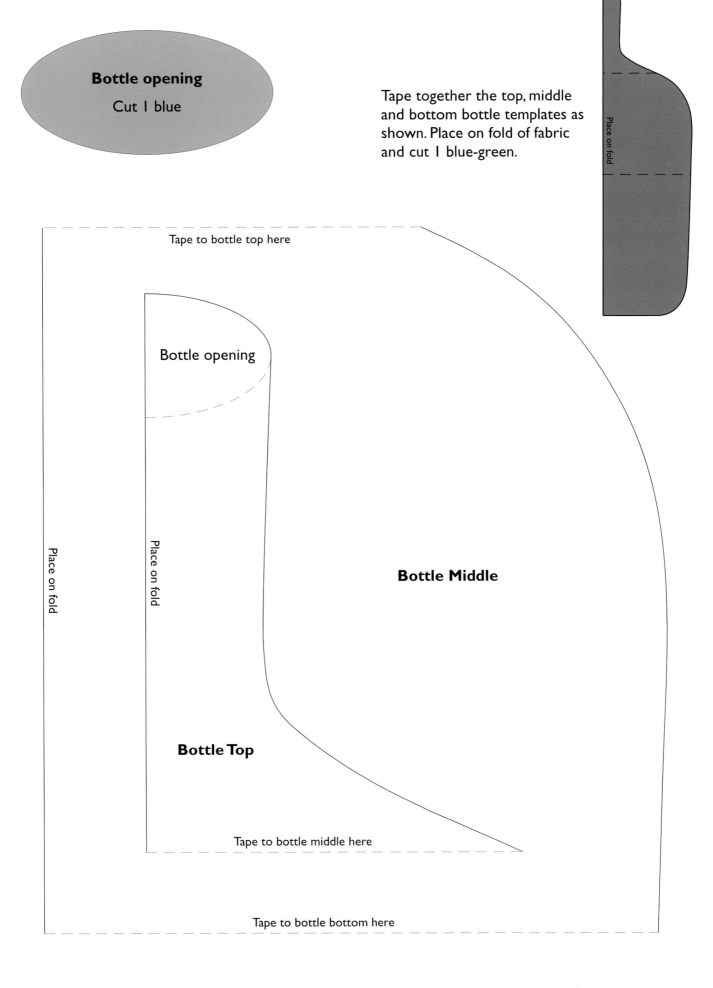

Bottle opening

Cut 1 blue

Tape together the top, middle and bottom bottle templates as shown. Place on fold of fabric and cut 1 blue-green.

Place on fold

Tape to bottle top here

Bottle opening

Place on fold

Place on fold

Bottle Middle

Bottle Top

Tape to bottle middle here

Tape to bottle bottom here

Tape to bottle middle here

Bottle Bottom

Place on fold

Short Mast
Cut 1 brown

Tall Mast
Cut 1 brown

Tape to bottle middle here

Grain wagons transported settlers moving west.

Underground Railroad

"Underground Railroad"
12" square
Stitched by Jean Stanclift

Before Abraham Lincoln was elected president and the War Between the States was fought, individuals, church groups, and intellectuals protested slavery through printed broadsides, tracts, anti-slavery fairs, and a newspaper called The Liberator. These people were called "abolitionists. They appealed to the American people and the United States government to put an end to the inhumane practice of owning slaves.

To avoid slave-made cotton, Quaker women wore silk dresses and made their quilts from silk. Abolitionists created a way to help runaway slaves coming out of the South, and give them safe escort to Canada where slave hunters were forbidden to enter. This plan was called the Underground Railroad.

Safe houses harbored escaping slaves, provided food, clothes, and a place to rest before slaves were guided to the next safe house. There was not just one road, but many routes leading people north so not to arouse suspicion among the slave catchers. Men and women who helped guide and transport slaves were called "conductors."

One woman, Harriett Tubman, walked off her owner's plantation and trusted God to guide her to a safe house. She reached safety in Pennsylvania, but instead of forgetting her family that she left behind, she went back to the South an estimated nineteen times. She brought her elderly parents and brothers, and led over 300 people to safety, in the north and Canada. Harriett baked pies for a hotel to help finance her trips, and made friends with Union government officials that gave her traveling money.

After the Civil War ended, women and girls made quilts that sold at fairs that raised money for widows and orphans. Quiltmakers remembered the terrible years of war with their needles and thread. This pattern came to be called "Underground Railroad" by Ruth Finley in 1929. It serves as a reminder of the long and dangerous effort by white and black people who set aside their own safety to help the bravest of all: the slaves who made the decision to escape enslavement.

Crazy quilt sewing machine advertising trade card.

FABRIC REQUIREMENTS

❋ White or ecru shirting or a neutral

❋ Brown

❋ Red

❋ Blue

CUTTING DIRECTIONS

For rotary cutting: Cut on the cross grain.

❋ Piece A: Cut 1 strip 2 1/2" wide of blue and 1 strip 2 1/2" wide of red. Cut the strips into 2 1/2" squares for 5-four patch squares.

❋ Piece B: Cut 1 strip 4 7/8" wide of white and 1 strip of 4 7/8" wide of brown. Cut 2 squares of each color. Cut the squares from corner to corner on the diagonal to make 4 triangles of white and four triangles of brown.

SEWING DIRECTIONS

Refer to the picture for color placement. Underground Railroad is constructed as a nine patch. Sew 2 red and 2 blue squares (piece A), together to make a four patch. You will need to make 5 four-patch blocks. Sew the brown and white triangles together to make half-square triangle blocks (piece B). Make 4 of the half-square triangle blocks. Sew all pieces together as shown in the diagram.

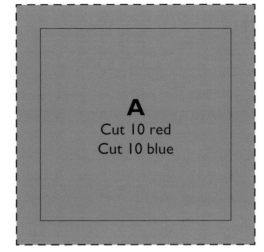

A
Cut 10 red
Cut 10 blue

B
Cut 4 white
Cut 4 brown

Piecing the block

Jacob's Ladder Table Cloth

Jacob's Ladder was another name for the Underground Railroad pattern.
Read all directions before beginning.

FABRIC REQUIREMENTS

(Makes 2 - 12" finished blocks.)

🔹 1 fat quarter each blue calico and a brown calico for 5 four-patch squares for piece A

🔹 1 fat quarter each small ecru print and a medium red for B triangles

🔹 5/8 yard of a large red print for 2 large setting triangles and corner triangles

🔹 1 1/4 yards for backing and borders. Karalee chose a brown wavy stripe to achieve the wavy edge of the border.

CUTTING DIRECTIONS

🔹 Cut 1 - 18 1/4" setting square and cut on diagonal both ways.

Cut 2-9 3/8" squares for corners, then cut from corner to corner on the diagonal.

BORDERS

🔹 Cut 2 - 4 1/2" x 42" for the top and bottom borders of table cloth and 2 - 4 1/2" x 25" for the end borders

🔹 Cut the backing 2" larger than the front.

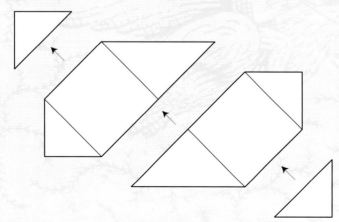

SEWING DIRECTIONS

🔹 Refer to the Underground Railroad block directions on page 56.

🔹 Piece 2 blocks as shown.

🔹 Set 2 blocks on point with the large triangles.

≈ Set the 4 corner triangles as shown.

≈ Cut 2 strips of brown stripe on the crossgrain from selvedge to selvedge, or the direction of the weave or stripe.

≈ Sew top and bottom, and side borders to the set blocks.

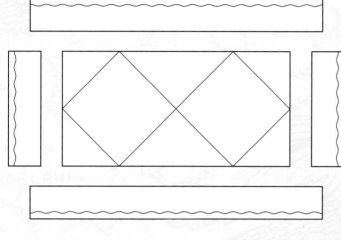

≈ DO NOT cut waves yet. If you want to miter the corners, add 10" more to the length of the side borders. Press all seams.

≈ With right sides together, pin front and back, leaving an opening for turning.

≈ Sew around the waves with a 1/8" seam allowance and with an open presser foot. It's easier to see the lines of the waves. Follow the wave line and cut excess fabric, leaving a 1/8" seam allowance. Use a pin or seam ripper to hold edges down as you sew, to prevent the fabric from rippling.

≈ Turn and push out a few waves with a point turner, then press, turn a few waves, then press. Repeat all around the border.

≈ After waves are pressed, stitch in the ditch between the wave seam allowances and the blocks.

"Jacob's Ladder" Table Cloth
23" x 40"
Stitched by
Karalee Fisher

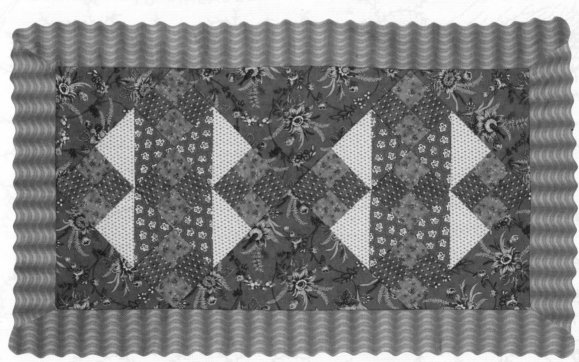

G.A.R.

"Grand Army of the Republic"
12"square
Stitched by Jean Stanclift

On Memorial Day as you walk through any cemetery in the United States, look at the headstones for a carved five-pointed star, or a metal star engraved with the letters G.A.R. stuck into the ground beside the headstone. G.A.R. stood for the Grand Army of the Republic. The end of the Civil War in 1865 brought men and boys home from the war and the country shifted its focus from war to rebuilding the lives and the land for the survivors.

Women now focused their sewing on raising money for orphans and widows, and providing homes for old soldiers. The G. A. R. and its female organization, the Women's Relief Corps, worked with families and veterans to restore a normal life to a country that was torn apart for four years.

Again, the needles and thread patched up the country by sewing comforters for wounded men. In the later years former first lady, "Julia Grant, headed the Women's National War Relief Association during the Spanish American war. Supplies and the comforters were sent by a hospital ship to Manila. Mrs. Grant advocated scholarships for soldier's children." -- Ishbel Ross, The General's Wife.

FABRIC

- 🐚 White shirting or neutral for the 12 1/2" square background
- 🐚 Red
- 🐚 Blue
- 🐚 Scrap of red stripe for flag
- 🐚 Scrap of blue star fabric for canton
- 🐚 Scrap of red or brown for flagpole

CUTTING DIRECTIONS

🐚 With red and blue fabric, sew a 2 1/2" x 24" strip with right sides together using a 1/4" seam allowance. Cut 5 rectangles 2 1/2" x 4 1/2"

🐚 Place the star point template with the line placed over the seam of the rectangles. Draw around the star points. Cut out each point adding a 1/4" seam allowance as you cut.

Union veteran and son. Note quilt on father's lap. He may have been living in a soldier's home supported by the G.A.R. (Photo courtesy of the Douglas County Historical Society)

Repeat for flag, canton, and circle, being sure to add the 1/4" seam allowance.

Cut out a 12 1/2" square for background.

SEWING DIRECTIONS

Place background on point and gently finger-press a line from top corner to bottom corner as a guide for placing the star point.

Appliqué the canton to the flag and the flag to the pole

Place the finished flag in the center of the circle, pin and appliqué. Baste under the seam all around the circle.

Center the circle over pieced stars, lining up the flag and star point. Refer to the picture. Pin and baste. Appliqué the circle to the star. (The circle might go a little above the dotted line on the star point pattern. Just be sure that the pieced star corners are well covered by the circle.)

Appliqué the star to the background block.

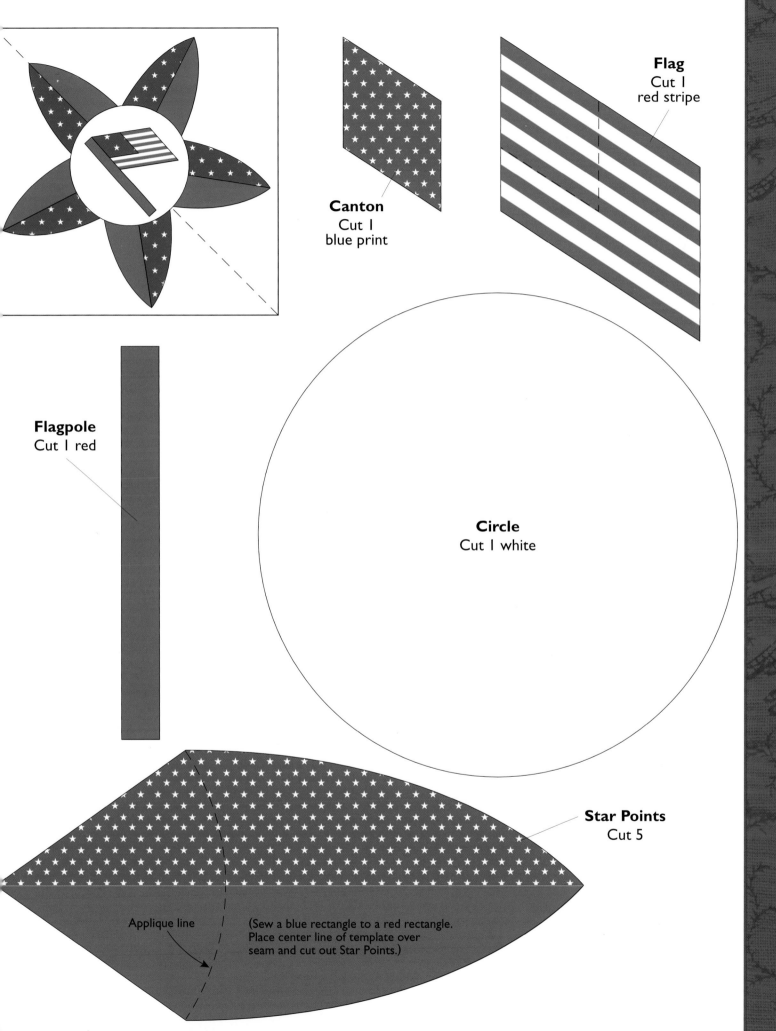

Canton
Cut 1
blue print

Flag
Cut 1
red stripe

Flagpole
Cut 1 red

Circle
Cut 1 white

Star Points
Cut 5

Applique line

(Sew a blue rectangle to a red rectangle. Place center line of template over seam and cut out Star Points.)

Star Pincushion

Stitched by Terry Thompson

G. A. R.
Calico Star Pincushion

YARDAGE
❋ 1 fat quarter pink for front
❋ 1 fat quarter brown print for back.
❋ 1 large or medium button
❋ Stuffing--wool roving or poly

CUTTING
❋ Use the star template and cut out 5 star points, adding a 1/4" seam allowance.

SEWING DIRECTIONS
Shorten the stitch length for strong seams.
❋ Piece the stars from the center raw edge to the outside corners, leaving a 1/4" open seam on each corner. See the dots on the diagram at the top of the next page for easy sewing and turning.
❋ Press seams to one side.
❋ Place the star face down on the backing with the right sides together. Pin in place. Cut out the backing following the shape of the star.
❋ Leave a 2 1/2" opening as you sew the backing and star together to insert stuffing. See dots on pattern (• opening •)
❋ Stuff firmly. Sew the opening closed.
❋ Sew a medium sized button in the star center, pulling front and back tightly together.

Lest we forget

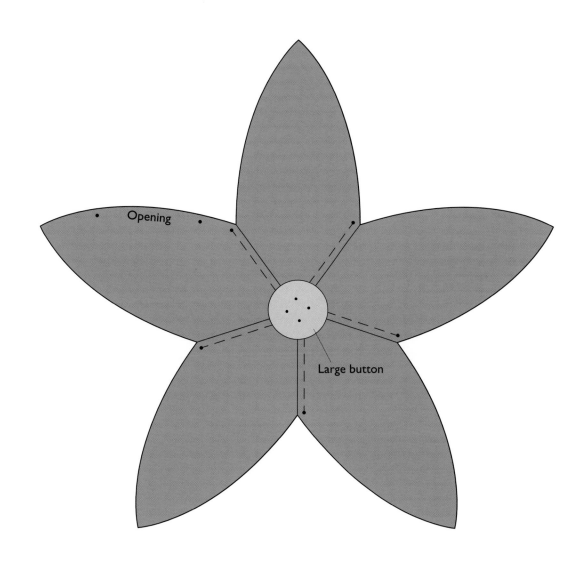

Opening

Large button

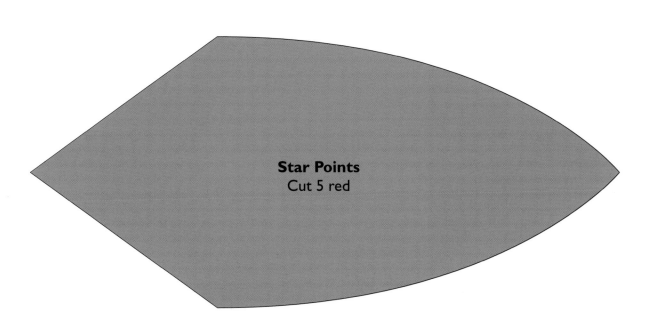

Star Points
Cut 5 red

WCTU Pledge

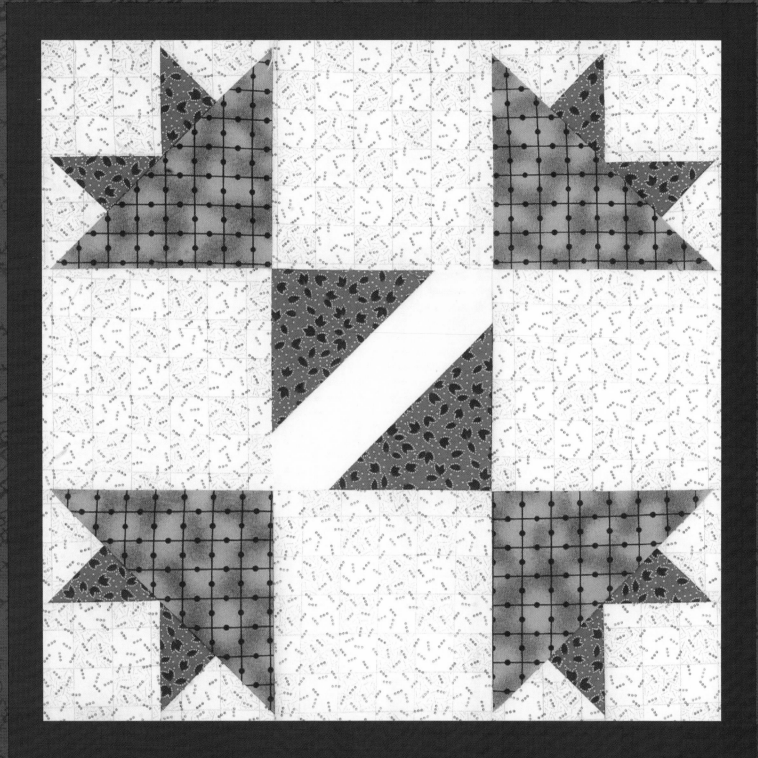

"WCTU Pledge"
12" square
Sewn by Jean Stanclift

For almost two centuries in America, women and children suffered from the effect of their husbands' and fathers' alcoholism. Paychecks didn't make it home on Friday. Verbal, sexual and physical abuse resulted in broken homes and lives.

In 1873, hundreds of women decided to take on this problem and do something about it. In December 1873, the Women's Temperance Crusade staged a protest march in Ohio. Out of that march came a flood of support from women from the Midwest who formed the Women's Christian Temperance Union, W.C.T.U.

Frances Willard became the second president of the Union and received letters from women from countries all over the world who also supported the goals of the Union.

The WCTU campaigned for other causes as well--votes for women, support for widows and orphans, dress reform and prison reform--using signature quilts to raise funds for their programs.

THE GENERAL OFFICERS OF THE WORLD'S W.C.T.U.

From Quilted All Day: The Prairie Journals of Ida Chambers Melugin, By Carolyn O'Bagy Davis, Tucson: Sampete Publications, Inc., 1993

"I done some mending and in the evening we all went to Church to hear the Temperance Lecture it was just fine." (9/11/1902) "done up our chores and went over to the lecture Lulu come home with us to go to the Church. It was a grand talk to young men there was a good many signed the pledge." (Thanksgiving Day, 11/27/1902).

FABRIC

- White or ecru shirting for background
- Red
- Blue
- Contrasting white scrap

ROTARY CUTTING INSTRUCTIONS

- Piece A: Cut 4 white 2 1/2" squares
- Piece B: Cut 4 - 3 1/4" squares, 2 red and 2 white. Cut squares in half on the diagonal and then in half again to give you 16 triangles.

- Piece C: Cut 4 white 4 1/2" squares.
- Piece D: Use template to cut white piece.
- Piece E: Cut 1 - 3 7/8" red square. Cut in half diagonally.

- Piece F: Cut 2 - 4 7/8" blue squares. Cut in half on the diagonal.

SEWING DIRECTIONS

- Sew dark and light B triangles together, being careful to make them mirror images.
- Sew white piece A to red and white B triangles, matching the outside edge, sewing from outside seam to inside. See piecing diagram on facing page.
- Sew A/B triangle unit to blue F triangle as shown.
- Sew E pieces to each side of D to make the center square. It will look as though E and D don't fit, but center the middles of each piece, pin and sew. It will fit.
- Sew all units in rows as you would a nine-patch block.

Freedom of Choice – Solving the Old Maid's puzzle.

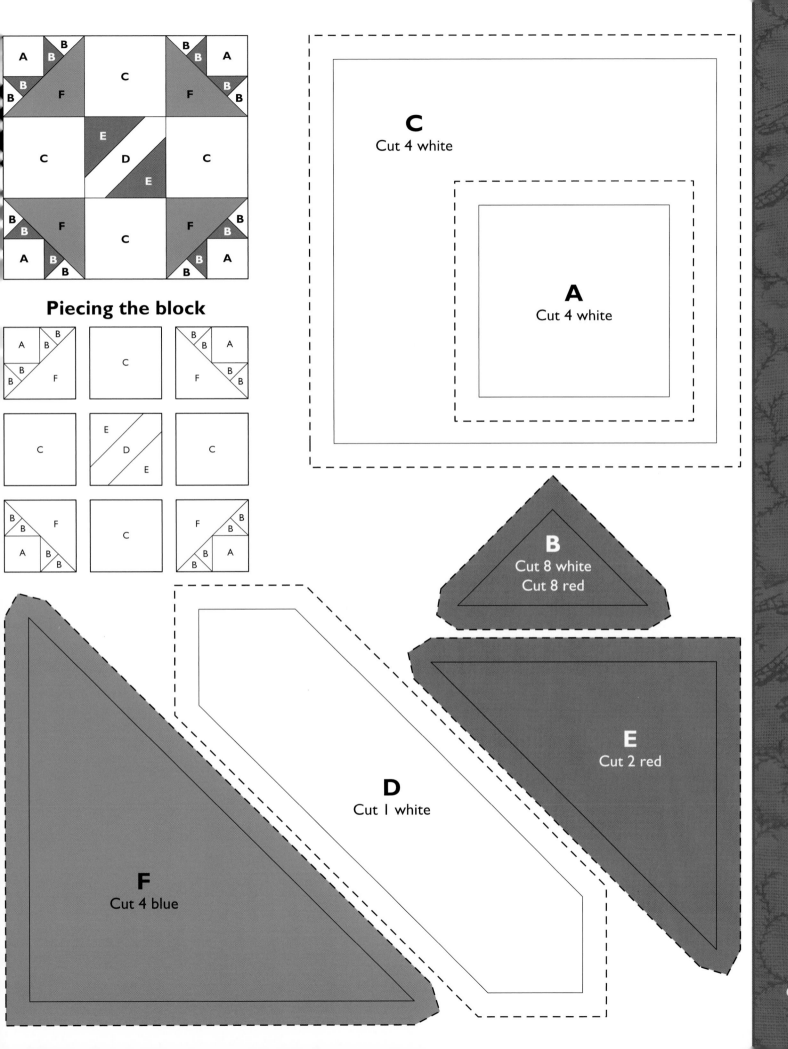

Piecing the block

C
Cut 4 white

A
Cut 4 white

B
Cut 8 white
Cut 8 red

E
Cut 2 red

D
Cut 1 white

F
Cut 4 blue

WCTU Pledge block pillow

FABRIC REQUIREMENTS

- 14" square pillow form
- 1 fat quarter of blue print
- Scrap of solid white
- 1/2 yd of white shirting for block, binding and backing
- 1/8 yd of black print of 1 1/2" border (finished to 1")
- A Pigma permanent pen in black for writing on the pillow

The binding has the appearance of piping, but Karalee's method is so much easier. She calls it "Quilter's Piping."

SEWING DIRECTIONS

- If you wish, sign your name in the center piece (D) or write WCTU by using a Pigma permanent pen in black, before sewing pillow.
- Follow the directions for the WCTU block on page 68.
- Sew a 1 1/2" black border around the edges of the block.
- Baste a 14 1/2" square of cotton batting to the back of the block.

BACKING

- Cut 2 pieces of backing 14" x 10" and sew a 1/4" hem on edge of each piece.

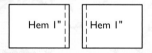

- With wrong sides together, lay block and back together, overlapping backs to fit the pillow top. Sew around pillow and backing. Turn cover inside out.
- Cut 2" wide strips for binding, cut on the straight grain.
- Bind front and backing as you would a quilt.
- Place pillow form inside pillow.

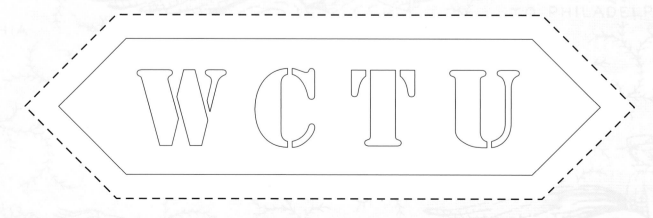

70

"WCTU Pledge" Block Pillow
14" square
Stitched by Karalee Fisher

Frances E. Willard in her Den Rest Cottage, 1890

Women's Pavilion

"Women's Pavilion"
12" square
Stitched by Jean Stanclift

The Women's Pavilion at the Centennial Exhibition in 1876 displayed the needle art of women who entered their quilts, embroidery, crochet and knitted projects for this great event. Thousands of women visited the Pavilion dedicated only to womens' arts and interests. Inspired by what they saw, many returned home and made their own Centennial quilt in honor of our country's 100th birthday. A good number of these quilts have the dates 1776-1876 appliquéd or embroidered in a prominent place on the quilt.

In G. Knappenberger's pieced Feathered Star center block, she appliquéd "1876" and the words above her name on the border spell "CENTENNIAL" in very large letters. Her joyful quilt, made in Pennsylvania contains hearts, lilies, baskets with birds, tulips and stars.

A quilt made in Ohio by Maria Whetstone Hallert contains pieced and point stars, an appliquéd eagle in the center and the dates "1776-1876" along with her name and the words appliquéd in the borders," This is the Centennial year - 1876," "From Washington to Grant," and "One hundred years."

An album quilt made by Minnie Burdick from North Adams, Massachusetts, in 1876, contains an appliquéd block of the Women's Pavilion and another block featuring banners stating "Declaration of Independence" and Centennial Anniversary - 1776-1876," flying over the Agricultural Hall.

Terry's Liberty quilt on page 4 was made in 1986 after the 100th birthday of the installation of the Statue of Liberty celebrated in New York City. "I saw 50 or more quilts displayed and came home and made my own Statue of Liberty quilt." - Where Liberty Dwells, There is my Country."

We are all influenced and moved by historical events, and some of us are compelled to record our memories of those events by stitching a quilt.

73

FABRIC

- White shirting for the background
- Small piece of brown for two flag poles 1/4" x 2 1/2"
- Small piece of green for a center stem, 1/4" x 3 1/2", 2 large leaves (#2) and 4 small leaves (#1), and 2 curved stems
- Small piece of red for 2 buds and 3 tulip centers
- 6" x 10" rectangle of reddish-brown striped print for basket and handle
- Small piece of red and white stripe for 2 flags, 5" x 3"
- Small piece (5" square) of blue star print for 2 cantons and 3 tulip calyx

CUTTING DIRECTIONS

- Cut a 12 1/2" square for background
- Trace patterns on template plastic or freezer paper and prepare for hand or machine appliqué.

SEWING DIRECTIONS

- Fold background block from corner to corner on the diagonal. Gently finger-press the fold. The fold line serves as a layout guide.
- Appliqué the small units together first before laying them on the block.
- Lay basket and handle in the center of the square. The bottom of the basket is 3 1/2" from the bottom corner and the handle is 3 1/2" from the top corner. Pin in place.
- Lay out pattern pieces as shown. Baste in loose stitches to hold in place for appliqué. Use a top running stitch.

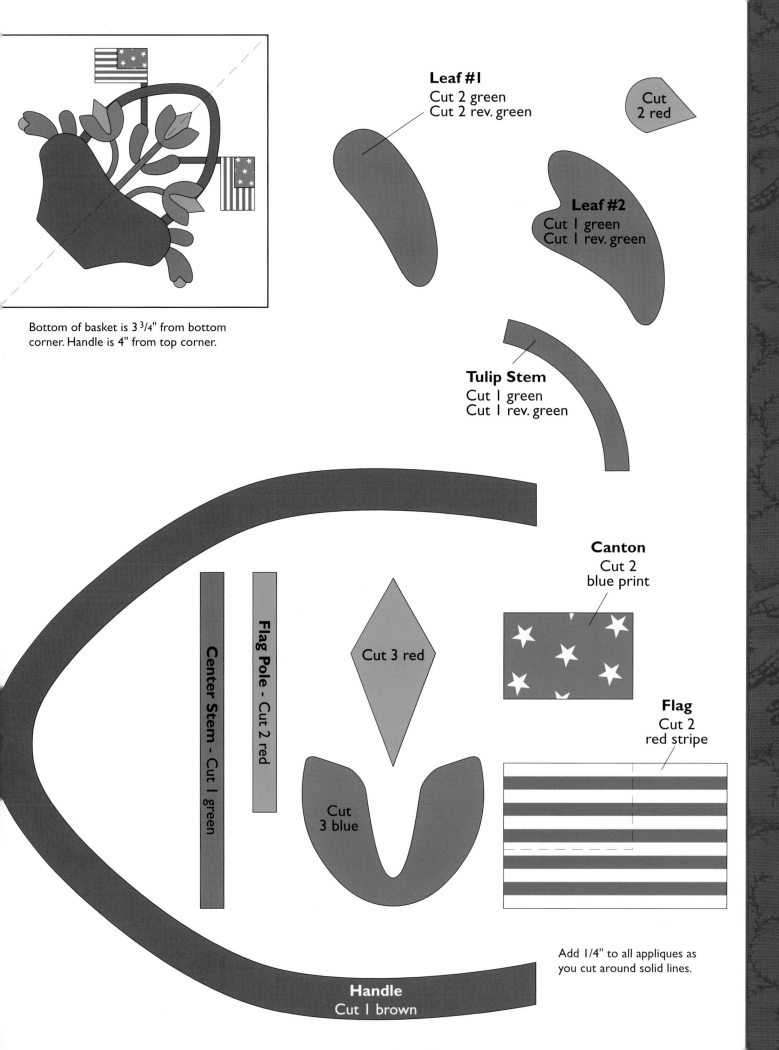

Leaf #1
Cut 2 green
Cut 2 rev. green

Cut
2 red

Leaf #2
Cut 1 green
Cut 1 rev. green

Bottom of basket is 3 ³/₄" from bottom
corner. Handle is 4" from top corner.

Tulip Stem
Cut 1 green
Cut 1 rev. green

Canton
Cut 2
blue print

Center Stem - Cut 1 green

Flag Pole - Cut 2 red

Cut 3 red

Cut
3 blue

Flag
Cut 2
red stripe

Add 1/4" to all appliques as
you cut around solid lines.

Handle
Cut 1 brown

Cut 1

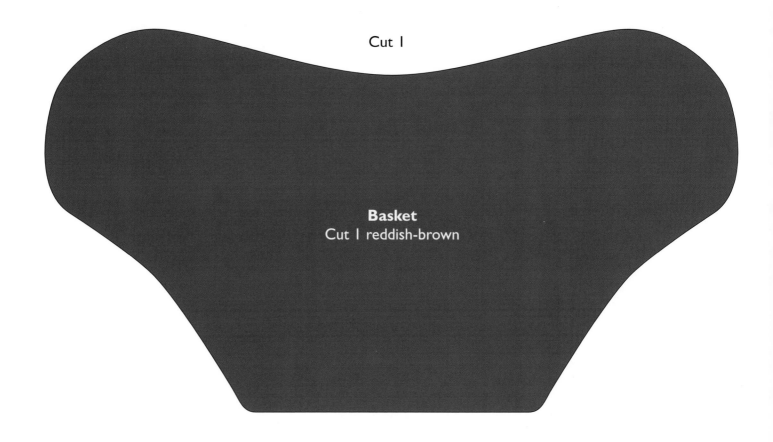

Basket
Cut 1 reddish-brown

Pressed Flower Picture - 9 1/2 x 13 1/2
Created by Terry Thompson

Women's Pavilion Pressed Flower Picture

YARDAGE

❧ 12" x 16" neutral or soft cream print for the background of the picture. Make it subtle so it will show off the flowers.

❧ Frame - My frame is 10" x 14" from the inside lip in back of frame. I like to use old, beat-up frames. If your frame is missing the glass, take your finished picture to a framer and have glass cut to fit your frame. You may use any size frame, just cut a piece of cardstock or foamcore that fits into the frame for the back of your picture.

❧ 1 fat quarter of a stripe, calico or any fabric that would make a nice basket and handle

❧ Freezer paper, approximately 10" square

❧ Roxanne's Glue-Baste It

❧ Masking tape

HOW TO PRESS FLOWERS
SUPPLIES

❧ Clean newspapers

❧ White copy paper

❧ Big books

❧ Corrugated cardboard, cut into 13" x 16" rectangles

❧ Your driest, least humid room

❧ Pointed toothpicks

❧ A small paper plate

❧ Glue stick

❧ Flowers - In the spring, use flowers that will lie flat, such as pansies, bleeding heart flowers, quince, old fashioned spirea, tickseed, buttercups, new green tree seedlings, sheeps grass, orange cosmos, coral bells, rose petals, or miniature roses. Take heavy stems off at the calyx. Pick your flowers by 11:00 a.m. so that the dew is gone and the color has risen into the blooms.

✻ Quickly layer an open newspaper with 1 sheet of white copy paper. Lay flowers face down over the copy paper.

✻ Place another sheet of paper over the blooms, close the newspaper and set it aside. Mold is the enemy. Make sure flowers rest in a dry place.

✻ Stack about 3 or 4 layers of newspaper on the floor or a place where there is good air circulation. Place a piece of corrugated cardboard between layers of 3-4 newspapers. Place a big book on top of the pile-or maybe two books.

✻ Leave undisturbed for about 2 weeks, take a peek to see if any have started to mold. Any moldy flowers should be thrown away.

✻ Leave the flowers in papers about 2 more weeks. If you open the papers and the flowers are flat and are easily moved, (the centers might stick, but just nudge them with your finger), they are ready for your picture.

✻ Press all wrinkles out of fabrics before you begin.

✻ Cover your foamcore with the background fabric. Stretch the edges of the fabric around the foamcore and glue stick it to the foamcore, folding corners inside corners.

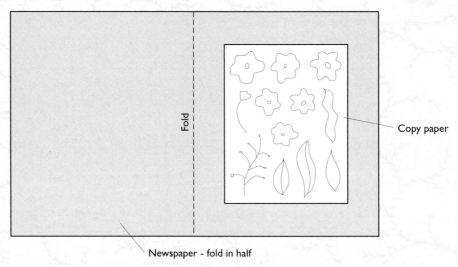

Fold

Copy paper

Newspaper - fold in half

❧ Draw basket and handle to the dull side of the freezer paper.

❧ Place shiny side of basket on wrong side of fabric. Turn under seam allowance and glue edges with glue stick.

❧ Cut out basket and handle, adding a 1/4" seam allowance as you cut. Prepare as you would for machine appliqué.

❧ Choose pressed flowers and group them according to colors. I like to keep pansies, and all flowers together as a group, just as you would in your garden. It makes a stronger statement than placing one or two flowers here and there.

❧ Make a "practice" picture before you glue down your flowers. Place the basket and handle in the center to make sure it will fit the frame.

❧ Place groups of flowers inside the handle and outside the basket as if they were picked and arranged that morning.

❧ Place greenery in first -- leaves, grasses, stems - as they will serve as a background.

❧ Layer two flowers together, create your own fantasy flowers.

❧ When you are satisfied with your picture, remove flowers.

❧ Using Roxanne's Glue-Baste It, glue basket and handle in place, leaving the top of the basket open so you can tuck some flowers inside.

Begin to glue each flower and leaf, one at a time with just a dot of Roxanne's Glue in the center of the back of the bloom. There is no need to glue the petals. I apply a little to stems, but the glass will hold everything in place. Use your imagination and fill the frame and basket with your flowers.

❧ Sign and date your picture.

❧ When you are finished, place clean glass into the frame, pick up your picture and place face down into the frame. Tape the picture to the frame until you can put in the nails or have a professional picture framer finish it with a hanger and brown paper over the back.

Temperance

"Temperance"
12"square
Stitched by Jean Stanclift

Women and girls pieced their T block at sewing circles, and the blue and white colors of the WCTU became the favored color scheme for the hundreds of blue and white Drunkards Paths quilts made from 1876-1920. I have a large collection of quilt blocks with many names and fabrics from the centennial years, 1876-1920, and the largest number of repeated quilt blocks are the pieced T blocks.

Crocheters voiced their opinions by crocheting the letter "T" and the words "Votes for Women" for the edgings of hand towels and tablecloths.

The world is a better place for women today, thanks to the hard work of our 19th and early 20th century mothers, grandmothers, and great grandmothers.

FABRIC

- ❀ White shirting or neutral for pieces A, B & D
- ❀ Indigo (navy) for pieces A and C

TEMPLATE PIECING

- ❀ Make plastic templates, label with the name of the pattern, color, letter and the number of pieces.
- ❀ Follow the steps in the example, piecing units together, and then in rows.

ROTARY CUTTING DIRECTIONS

❧ Piece A: Cut two navy 4 7/8" squares and cut each in half diagonally. Repeat in white.

Sew block using the diagram as a guide, sewing units together, then set in rows as you would a nine-patch.

❧ Piece B: Cut white strip 5 1/4" wide. Cut 2 - 5 1/4" squares. Cut each square from corner to corner on the diagonal.

❧ Piece C: Cut a strip of navy 2 7/8". Cut into 4 - 2 7/8" squares. Cut the squares from corner to corner on both diagonal lines to get 16 C triangles of navy.

❧ Piece D: Cut 1 white 4 1/2" square.

SEWING DIRECTIONS

❧ Sew units and then follow guide for setting in rows.

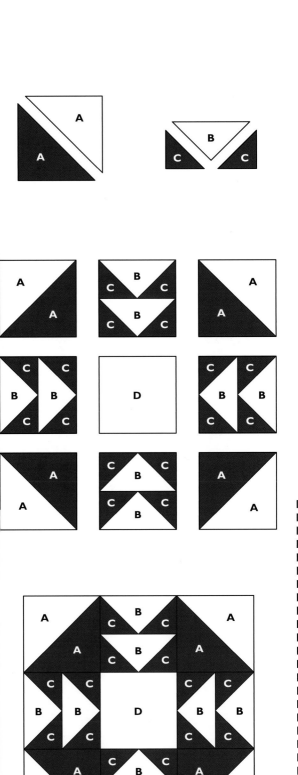

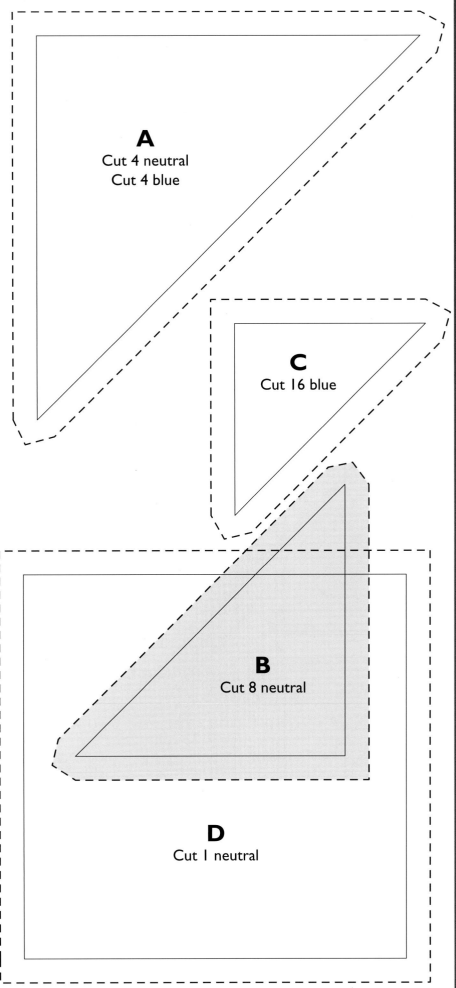

A
Cut 4 neutral
Cut 4 blue

C
Cut 16 blue

B
Cut 8 neutral

D
Cut 1 neutral

Temperance Crib Quilt

YARDAGE

This block is smaller and slightly different from the 12" blocks

- 1 yard indigo (navy) for 15 blocks, 8" finished blocks
- 1 yard white or ecru
- 5/8 yard for borders

TEMPLATE PIECING

- A: Cut 60 navy triangles, cut 60 white triangles
- B: Cut 120 white triangles
- C: Cut 300 navy triangles
- D: Cut 15 white squares

ROTARY CUTTING

- A: Cut 30 - 3 1/2" squares of navy and 30 - 3 1/2" squares of white. Cut squares on the diagonal to get 60 navy triangles and 60 white triangles.

- B: Cut 30 - 3 7/8" white squares, then cut from corner to corner on the diagonals to get 4 triangles from each square for 120 white triangles in all.

- C: Cut 150 - 2 1/8" squares of navy. Then cut from corner to corner on the diagonal to get 300 navy triangles.

- D: Cut 15 - 2 3/8" squares of white for center squares.

White ribbon recruits were the youth members of the Women's Christian Temperance Union.

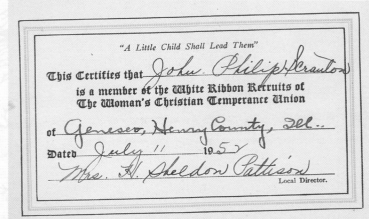

"A Little Child Shall Lead Them"

This Certifies that *John Philip Scranton* is a member of the White Ribbon Recruits of The Woman's Christian Temperance Union

of *Geneseo, Henry County, Ill.*

Dated *July 11* 19 5 *7*

Mrs. H. Sheldon Pattison

Local Director.

"Temperance" Crib Quilt

31" x 47"

Vintage T-Blocks set by Suzannah Christenson, Lawrence, Kansas

Quilted by Rosie Mayhew, Topeka, Kansas

TEMPERANCE

SEWING BLOCKS

✳ Use the graphic design as a guide for piecing the 15 blocks.

✳ Begin by piecing the center square, attaching 4 navy C triangles, to 1 white D square - 1 triangle to each side of D

✳ Sew navy and white A triangles for 4 corner squares

✳ Sew white B and navy C triangles as shown. Make 4 units.

✳ Now sew the pictured rows together as you would a nine patch block.

SETTING BLOCKS

✳ Set the blocks in 5 rows, 3 blocks per row. Refer to the picture.

✳ Cut borders 4" wide to finish at 3 1/2".

✳ Quilt in historical double lines, right over the pieced blocks.

✳ Bind in navy bias print

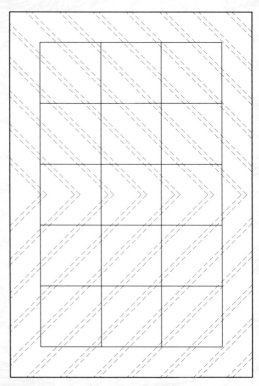

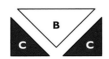

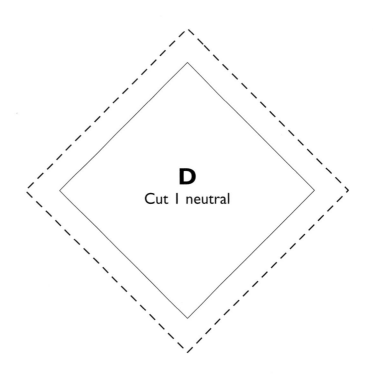

D
Cut 1 neutral

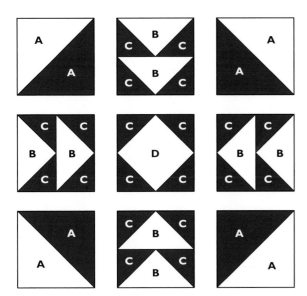

C
Cut 20
blue

A
Cut 4 neutral
Cut 4 blue

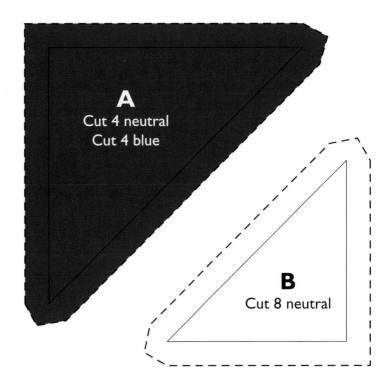

B
Cut 8 neutral

Pennsylvania Cutwork Snowflake

"Pennsylvania Cutwork Snowflake"
12" finished block
Stitched by Jean Stanclift

All through the 1800's, women sewed with family members, friends and neighbors. Once a week, sewing circles met at a church or home to quilt a member's quilt or to make special album quilt blocks. Each woman signed her name in brown ink, sometimes adding a date and a short verse of sentiment for the person receiving the block. The purpose of the album quilt varied, some were made for a couple's wedding, a minister and his wife who were leaving, or a family ready to pioneer the West.

The album blocks contain a theme of appliquéd vases holding lovely realistic flowering roses, lilies, Christmas cactus, ships surrounded by a floral wreath, houses, landmarks, hunting scenes, eagles with flags, liberty poles and caps, lyres, and anchors.

Pennsylvania Germans cut lovely paper valentines and used their skill cutting folded fabric four or eight times to produce an appliqué that looked like a snowflake.

This snowflake pattern has a small hole in the center--You can cut it larger if you like--for an inked name date or place.

FABRIC

- White shirting or neutral
- Red print for snowflake

CUTTING DIRECTIONS

- Cut a 12 1/2" background block.
- Press the lines as shown on the pattern, both solid and dotted.
- Cut a red 12 1/2" square for the snowflake.
- Fold the red fabric in half and then in half again on the solid lines. Lightly press. Fold again on dotted diagonal lines, press.
- Make a template of the snowflake.
- Draw around the template, on the folded square or move it around the square's pressed lines. Cut around lines with a 1/4" seam allowance. Cut out the hole in the center.

SEWING DIRECTIONS

- Appliqué onto the background block, lining up the points of the snowflakes with the pressed lines of the background block.

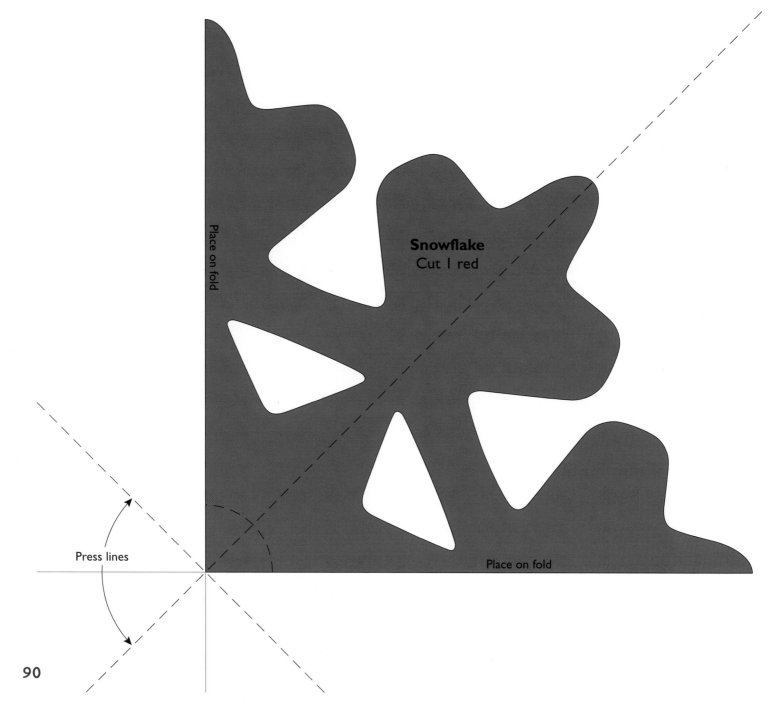

Place on fold

Snowflake
Cut 1 red

Place on fold

Press lines

Snowflake Hooked Rug

SUPPLY LIST

- 1/2 yard of monk's cloth
- 1/2 yard of mixed yellows for snowflake
- 3/4 yard of mixed blues for background
- 42" of 1 1/2" ecru twill tape
- Rug hook and frame
- 1/3 yd of fiberglass window screen
- Magic marker

DIRECTIONS

- Place screening over monk's cloth, centering the snowflake design on the screen
- With a magic marker, trace over the lines on the screening. The ink will bleed through the small holes in the screen and the design will then be transferred to the monk's cloth.
- Cut wool strips using a #6 cutter; for the yellow snowflake, use a cutter one size smaller. Some rug hookers cut wool with scissors or a rotary cutter and mat.
- Hook the interior design of the rug first, working out to the blue background, which is hooked last.
- Block the finished rug.
- Bind the edges with a wool yarn in an overcast stitch.
- To hide the raw edges, trim to 1" and cover the raw edge with a twill tape, sew down.

Always roll your rug with the design on the outside.

Snowflake Hooked Rug
13" x 13"
Hooked by Pam Mayfield
Lawrence, Kansas

Center Square

Libertyville quilt center square, and heart triangles
24" finished square
Stitched by Jean Stanclift

The large cornucopia looking figure holding flowers originated from an old symbol that represented freedom - the Liberty Cap. Throughout history, the cap held great meaning for people suffering oppression.

What is a Liberty cap and pole? Many people do not recognize this very historical image that appears in 19th century patriotic and political quilts. "The Phrygian" cap was a red knitted cap worn by freed slaves from Roman times, and worn by the French Revolutionaries. It symbolizes freedom from slavery and oppression and it usually is shown on top of a tall pole behind or held by the image of Liberty or Columbia. (Look at a silver dollar to see Liberty wearing a cap like this.) Colonial freedom fighters placed a Liberty pole and cap in the middle of the village square in protest to English laws and "taxation without representation."

Miss Liberty or Columbia, a symbol of liberty in Greek classical dress, appears in period paintings, needlework, and printed cotton textiles. She is usually portrayed sitting on a large rock with a shield at her feet and the Liberty pole and cap behind her. The Liberty cap is sometimes mistaken for a cornucopia in the appliquéd album quilts of the 1840's-1860's.

In many album blocks, the cap is made of rings of yellow, red, and blue, although many other blocks show the cap in turkey red, brown, gold, or madder red printed stripes.

Why does a Liberty cap have flowers, fruit and grains spilling forth in these blocks? "With Liberty comes abundance." says quilt historian Barbara Brackman.

The surrounding corner hearts represent Philadelphia, the City of Brotherly Love where the Centennial Exhibition of 1876 was held.

FABRIC

- Striped neutral or shirting for center
- Scraps of various colors
- Medium floral print for heart triangles

TO APPLIQUÉ CENTER SQUARE

- Cut out all appliqué pieces and prepare for hand or machine appliqué. Cut the center square 24 1/2". Lay the square on point.
- For center stem, cut bias strips 1" wide and use a Clover bias maker to turn edges in 1/4" for a finished 1/2" stem.
- Place the bottom of the Liberty Cap 5" from the lower point of the square.
- Place all appliqués, leaves, and stems by referring to picture. Tulip templates are in the Tulip Wheel chapter.

THE FOUR CORNER TRIANGLES WITH HEARTS

- See diagram
- Cut 2 - 17 7/8" squares each of the medium floral print. Cut both squares on the diagonal.
- Appliqué hearts and 1/4" x 9 1/2" bias stems to corner triangles.

- Sew corner triangles to each side of the square.

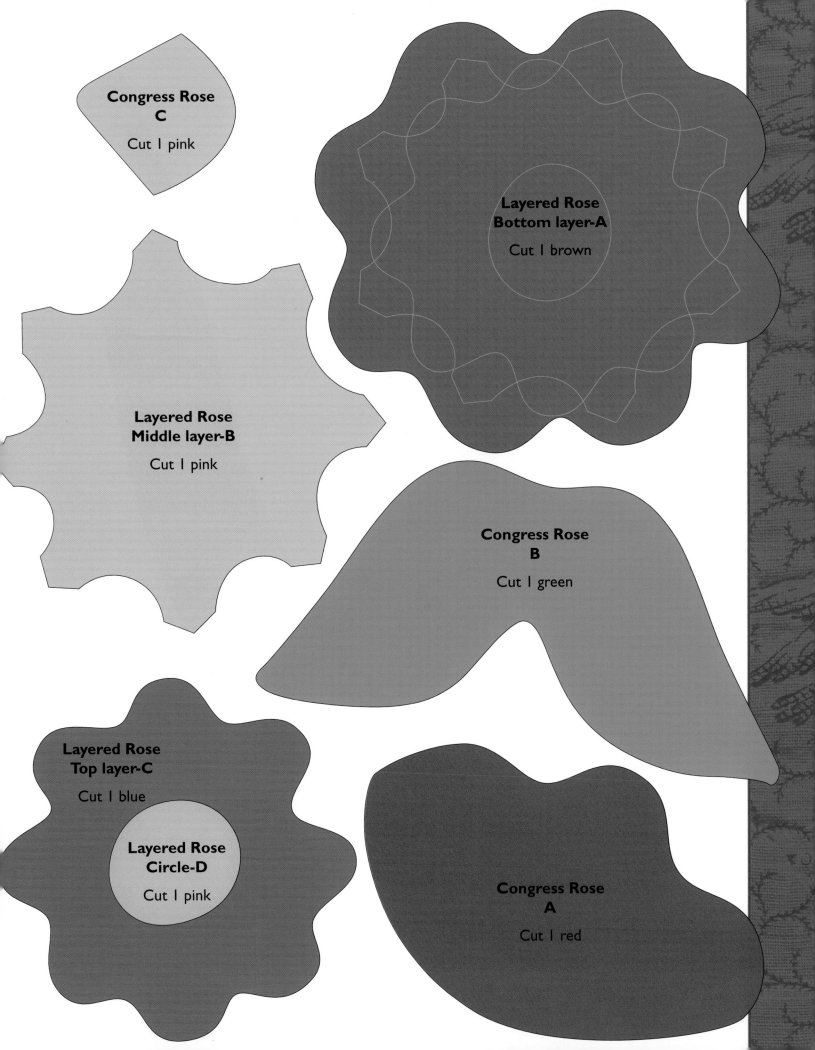

**Congress Rose
C**

Cut 1 pink

**Layered Rose
Bottom layer-A**

Cut 1 brown

**Layered Rose
Middle layer-B**

Cut 1 pink

**Congress Rose
B**

Cut 1 green

**Layered Rose
Top layer-C**

Cut 1 blue

**Layered Rose
Circle-D**

Cut 1 pink

**Congress Rose
A**

Cut 1 red

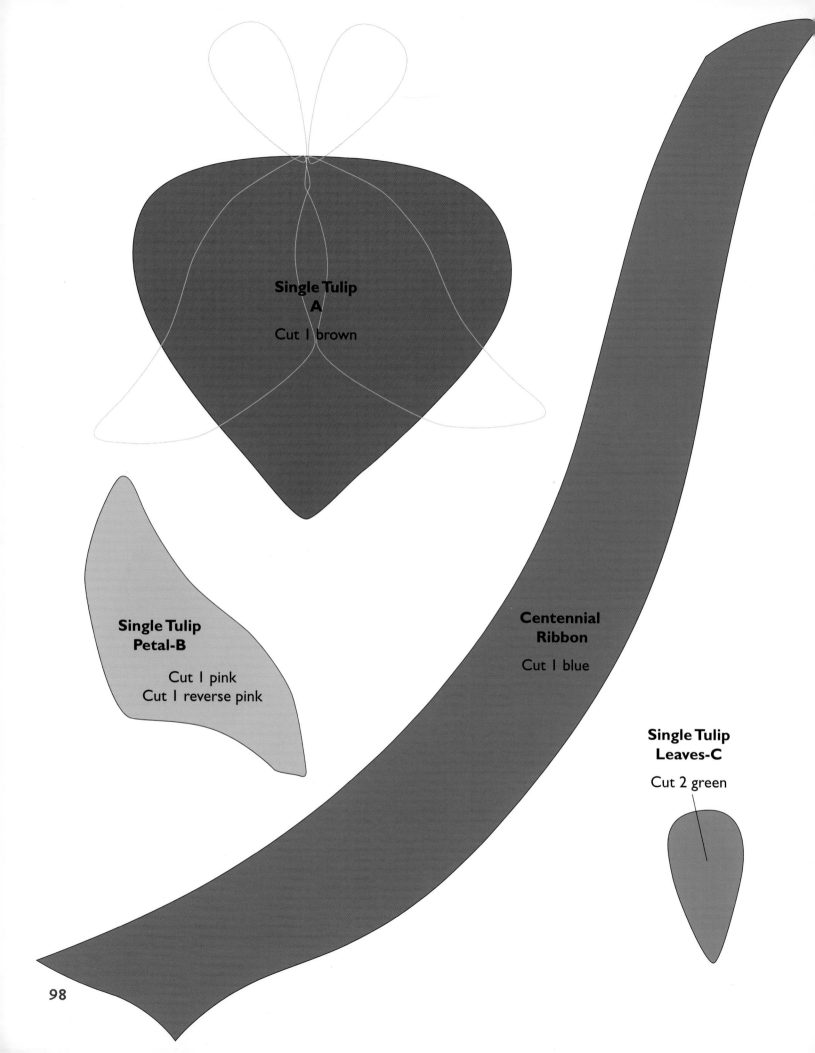

**Single Tulip
A**

Cut 1 brown

**Single Tulip
Petal-B**

Cut 1 pink
Cut 1 reverse pink

**Centennial
Ribbon**

Cut 1 blue

**Single Tulip
Leaves-C**

Cut 2 green

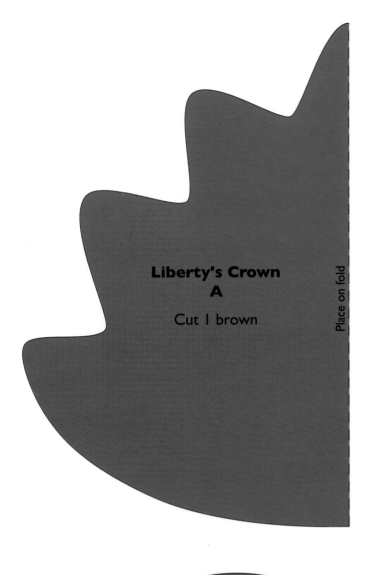

**Liberty's Crown
A**

Cut 1 brown

Place on fold

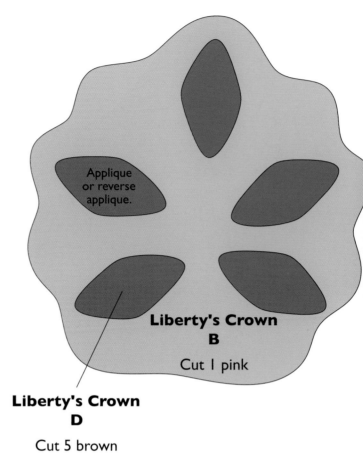

Applique
or reverse
applique.

**Liberty's Crown
B**

Cut 1 pink

**Liberty's Crown
D**

Cut 5 brown

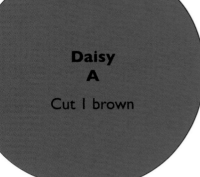

**Daisy
A**

Cut 1 brown

**Daisy
Stem-C**

Cut 1 green

**Daisy
Petal-B**

Cut 3 blue
Cut 2 brown

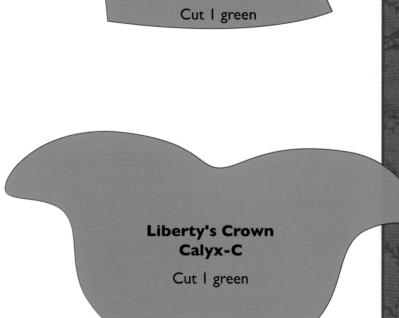

**Liberty's Crown
Calyx-C**

Cut 1 green

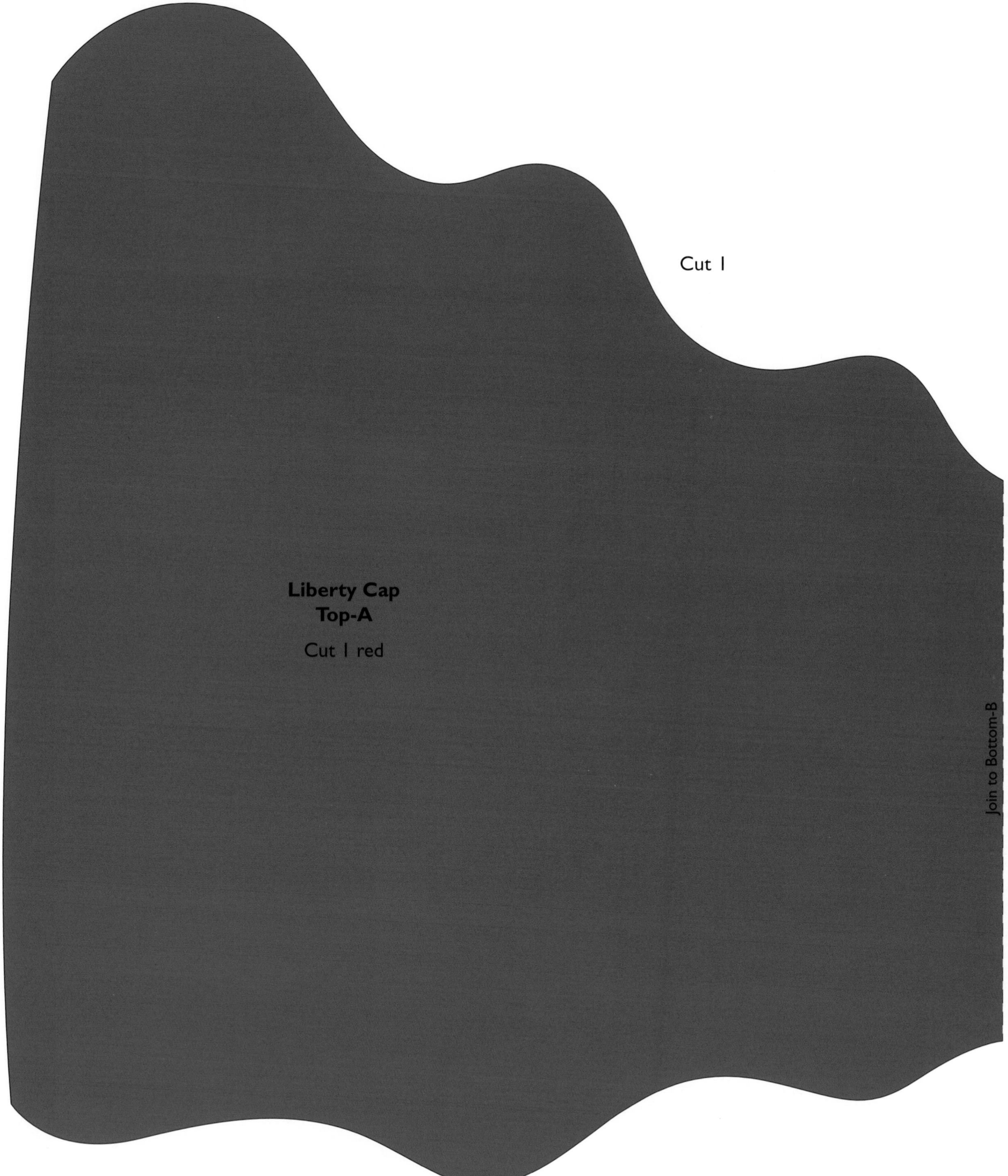

Cut 1

**Liberty Cap
Top-A**

Cut 1 red

Join to Bottom-B

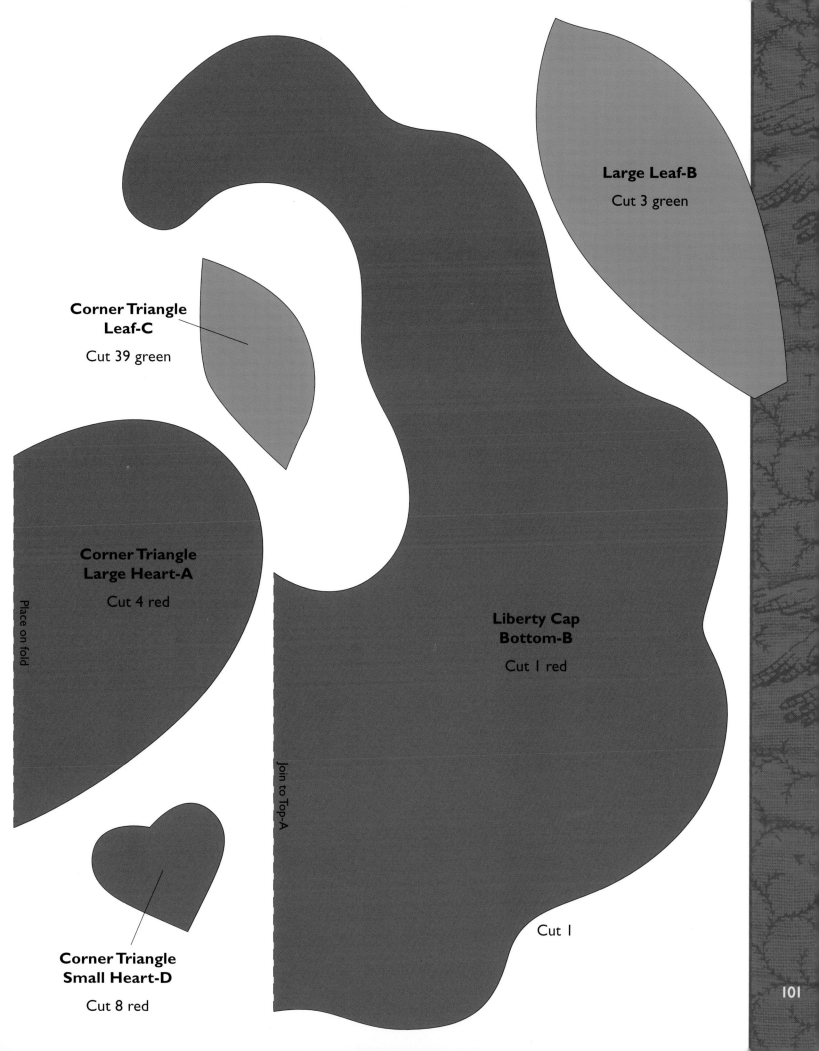

Large Leaf-B

Cut 3 green

**Corner Triangle
Leaf-C**

Cut 39 green

**Corner Triangle
Large Heart-A**

Cut 4 red

Place on fold

**Liberty Cap
Bottom-B**

Cut 1 red

Join to Top-A

Cut 1

**Corner Triangle
Small Heart-D**

Cut 8 red

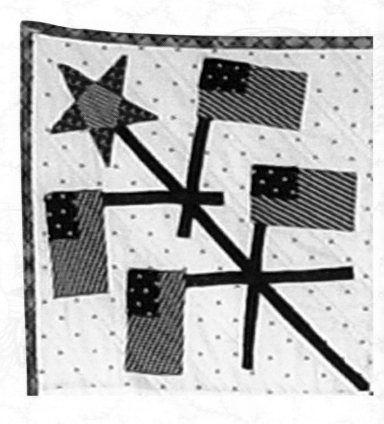

Borders and Corners

FABRIC REQUIREMENTS

❧ Scraps of brown, tan, red and white stripe, blue for eagle corners

❧ Scraps of dark brown, red and white stripe, blue with stars for flag squares

❧ 1 yard red calico, 1 yard blue calico for swags

❧ 1 fat quarter yellow for center of stars

❧ 3 yards of a white shirting or neutral for the 12" wide border background.

PREPARING EAGLE CORNERS

❧ Ink or embroider a black eye on each bird.

❧ Prepare appliqués for 2 eagles, log and federal shield.

❧ You may position eagles either standing on a log or flying with the shield. The templates are the same. Just arrange them referring to the picture on page 102, or to the diagram below.

❧ The 2 eagle and the 2 flag corners are each appliquéd on a 12 1/2" square. See diagrams on page 106.

❧ Cut corner blocks and borders from the same fabric.

PREPARING FLAG CORNERS

🌼 Use 1/2" Clover bias maker for turning 1/4" seam allowance. Cut strips on grain, not bias.

🌼 Cut 2 dark brown strips, 1" x 12 1/2" for center poles. Cut 4 - 1" x 4 1/2" strips for the top poles, and 4 - 1" x 5 1/2" strips for the bottom poles.

🌼 Cut 8 flags and 8 cantons. I placed the flag template so the stripes would be on the diagonal to give a feeling of movement.

PREPARING SWAG AND STAR BORDERS

🌼 For the top swag, cut 16 red print calico pieces. Cut 16 blue of the bottom swag.

🌼 Cut 22 yellow star centers and 14 red and 8 blue stars. Appliqué star center to blue and red stars.

🌼 Borders are cut on the cross grain and pieced together for 4 - 12 1/2" x 68 1/2" borders.

🌼 Baste top and bottom swags, stars, and cantons on flags. Place appliqué pieces on each border and corner square and sew.

PUTTING IT TOGETHER

Sew finished borders and squares to the body of the quilt. Sew the side borders first, then sew the top and bottom borders with the eagle and flag squares to the quilt.

QUILTING

Lori Kukuk quilted half feather wreaths in the large blue triangles. She echo quilted around the appliqués in the 6 blocks, the center square and heart triangle. For the pieced blocks, she quilted straight and double lines 1/4" x 1 1/4" apart.

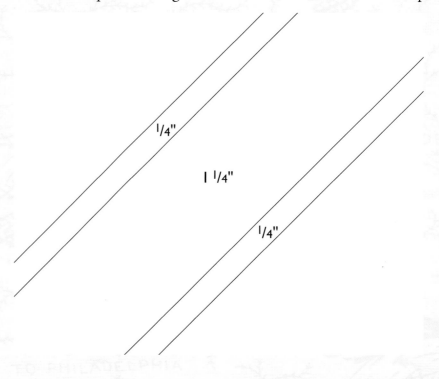

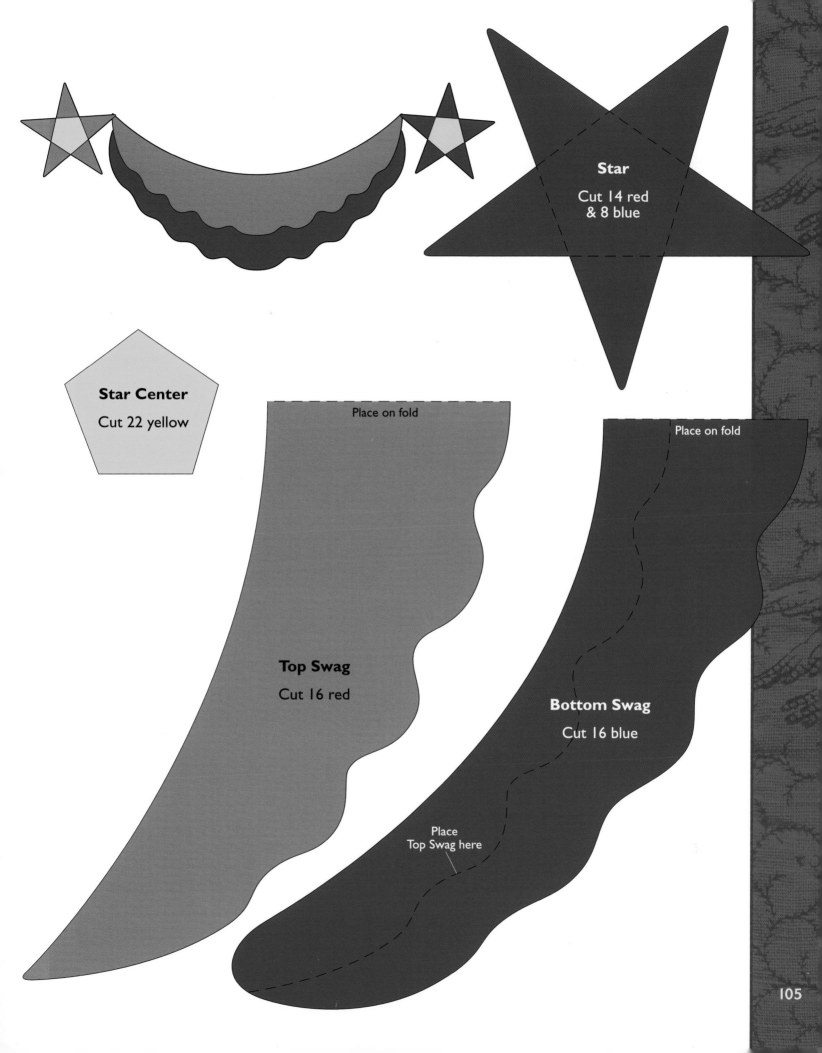

Star

Cut 14 red
& 8 blue

Star Center

Cut 22 yellow

Place on fold

Place on fold

Top Swag

Cut 16 red

Bottom Swag

Cut 16 blue

Place
Top Swag here

105

Eagle Body

Cut 2 brown

Left Leg
Cut 2 reverse tan

Right Leg
Cut 2 tan

Beak

Cut 2 tan

Applique
beak here

Eye is
embroidered

Eagle Head

Cut 2 tan

Tail

Cut 2 brown

106

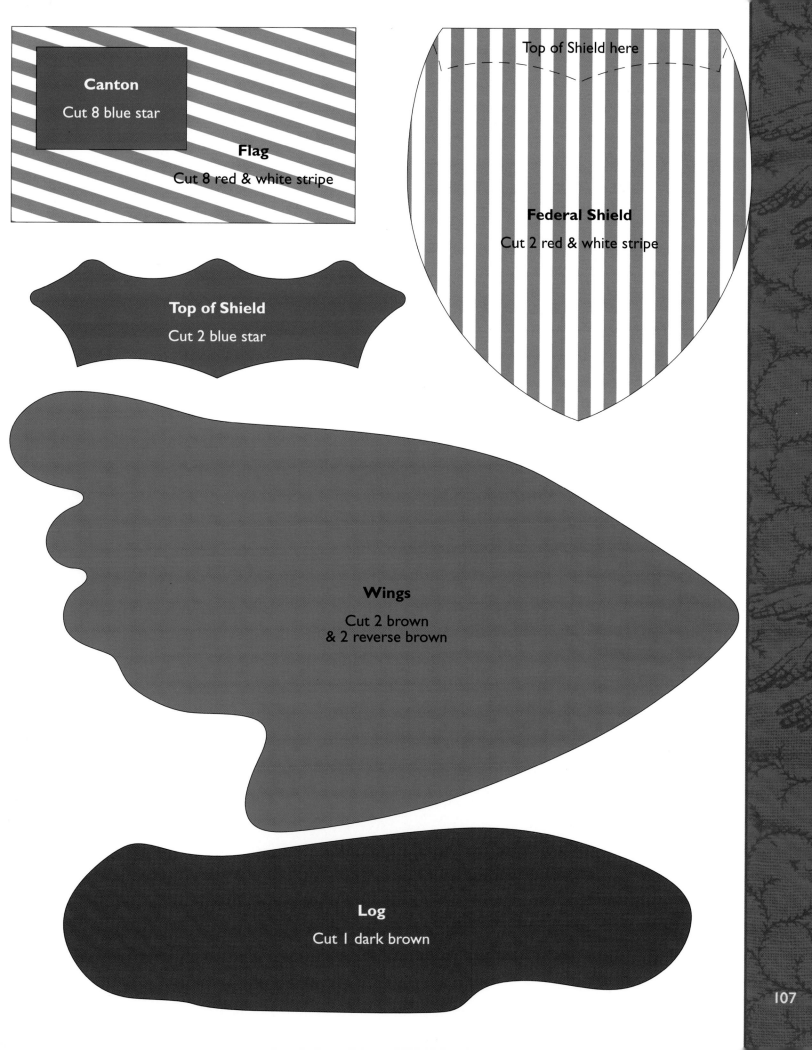

Canton
Cut 8 blue star

Flag
Cut 8 red & white stripe

Top of Shield here

Federal Shield
Cut 2 red & white stripe

Top of Shield
Cut 2 blue star

Wings
Cut 2 brown
& 2 reverse brown

Log
Cut 1 dark brown

Setting Side and Corner Triangles

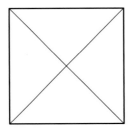

A. Cut 4 - 18 1/4" squares. Cut into 4 triangles to set blocks.

B. Cut 8 - 9 3/8" squares. Cut into 2 triangles for the corners of blocks.

Follow these diagrams for placement and setting blocks together.

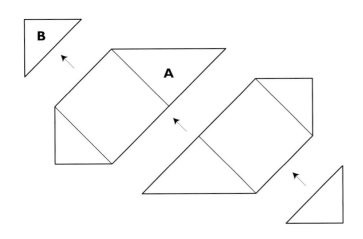

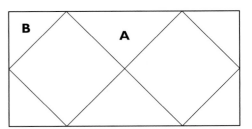

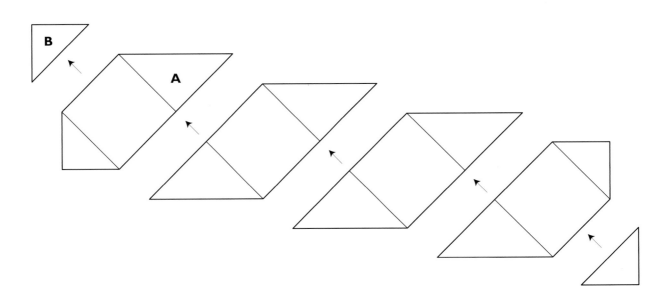

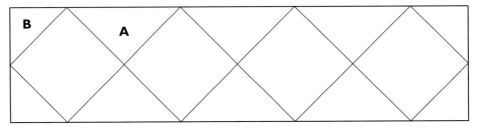

| 12" × 12" | 12" × 68" | 12" × 12" |

17"

B   A   A   A   B

12"

B   A   A   A   B

B   B

17"

| 12" × 68" | 8 ½"   A | 24" | 12" × 68" |

B   B

34"

| 12" × 12" | 12" × 68" | 12" × 12" |

92" × 92"

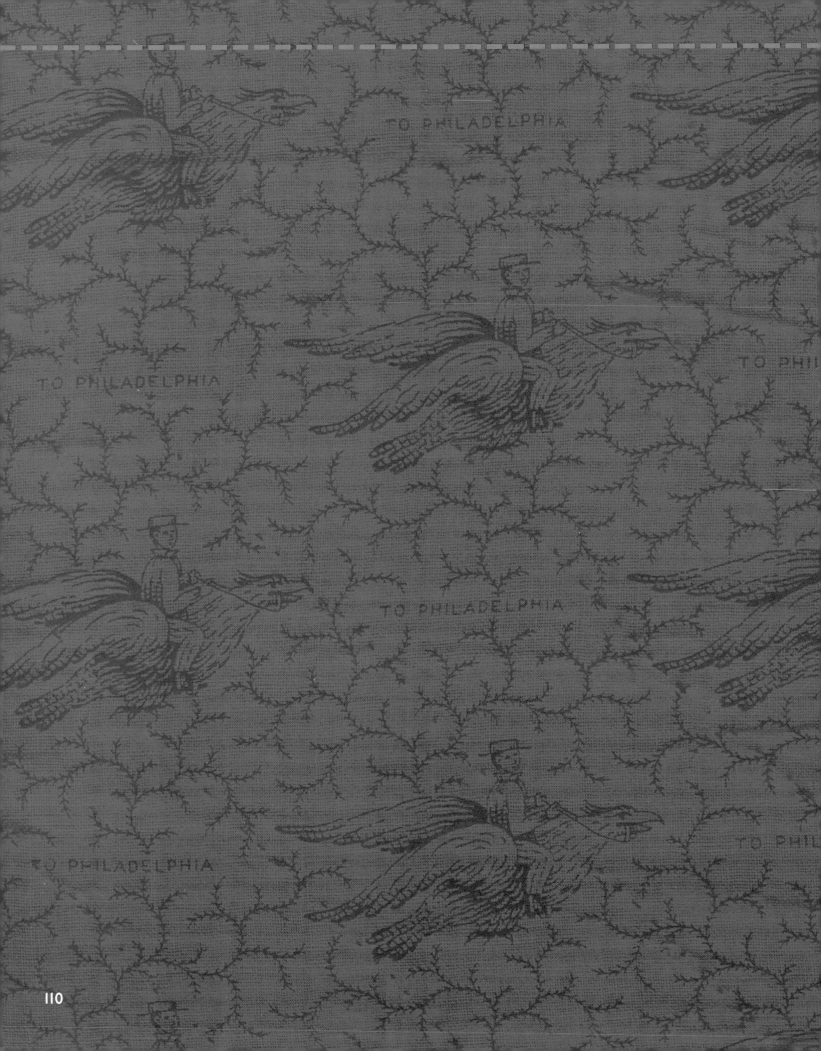

Blue Heart Pillow Cover with Lace

Blue Heart Pillow Cover
Size: 21" x 48"
Stitched by Jean Stanclift

Pillow covers simply lie over the pillows or the top of the sheet. This one is made to go with the New Centennial quilt on page 131.

FABRIC REQUIREMENTS

- 🌿 1 1/3 yards brown print, same as the Centennial quilt for background
- 🌿 1 1/3 yards red print for backing
- 🌿 1 1/4 yards red for star borders and 10 red hearts
- 🌿 1 fat quarter blue for 1 large and 10 small hearts
- 🌿 1/2 yard green for 1" bias stems
- 🌿 2 different scraps of green for 13 leaves
- 🌿 Use vintage lace for end pieces, or sew rows of different laces to a background, 18" x 21", and sew on each end of cover.

Refer to picture for placement.

CUTTING DIRECTIONS

- 🌿 Use freezer paper to trace the star border pattern the length of each border. Cut long borders 48 1/2" x 3 1/2" and 2 end borders 21 1/2" x 3 1/2". Adjust size to fit your bed or pillows. Iron freezer paper on back. Cut 4 strips. Tip: I overlapped the star points so that the freezer paper is connected. Cut out star borders adding a 1/4" seam allowance.
- 🌿 Cut 1" bias strips for vines. Use a 1/2" Clover bias maker to finish bias at 1/2" wide strips. Top vines measure 25" long, bottom measures 17" long.

SEWING DIRECTIONS

Machine or hand appliqué star borders to edges on top cover. Begin in the corners and fudge in the middle to make borders fit.

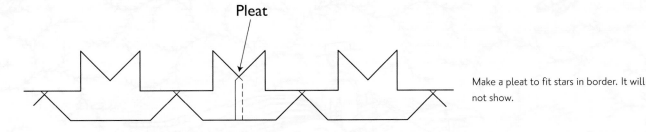

Pleat

Make a pleat to fit stars in border. It will not show.

- 🌿 Prepare all appliqués for machine or hand appliqué
- 🌿 Center large blue heart in center of background. Pin and baste.
- 🌿 Lay out vines, small hearts and leaves. Pin and baste.
- 🌿 Appliqué all pieces.
- 🌿 Trace date 1876, or your own name and year. Embroider with an outline stitch.
- 🌿 Sew lace borders to ends of covers.
- 🌿 With right sides together, sew front and back together, leaving an opening for turning. Turn, sew opening closed.

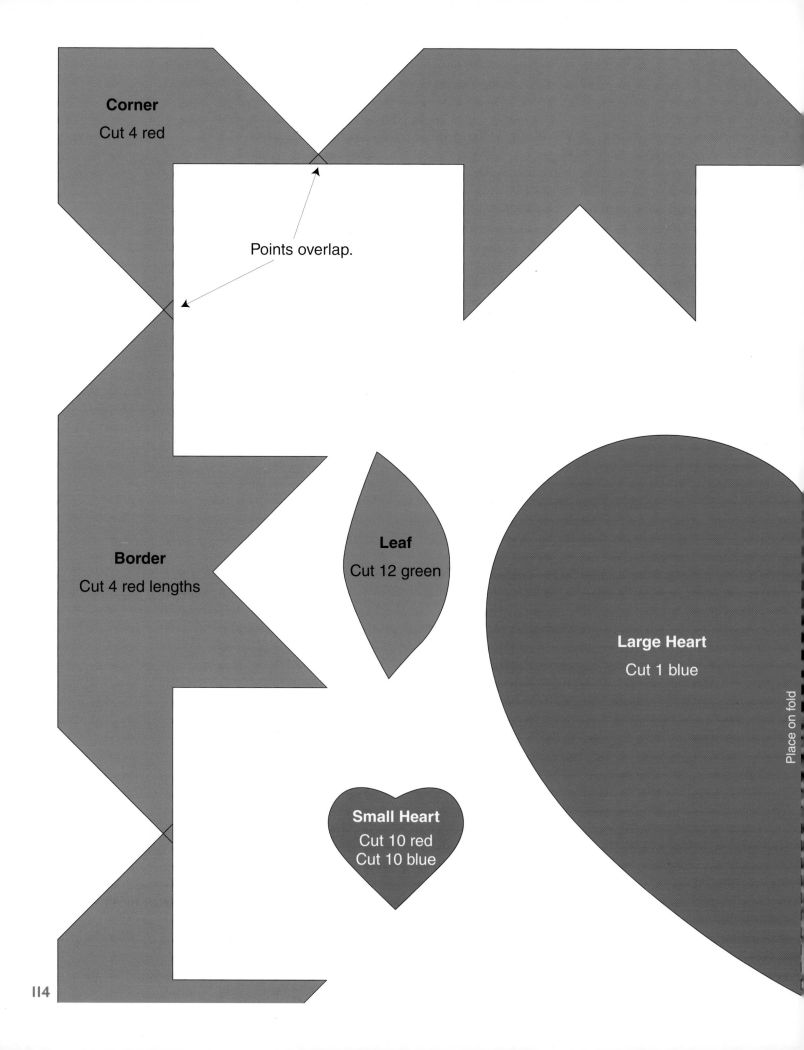

Corner
Cut 4 red

Points overlap.

Border
Cut 4 red lengths

Leaf
Cut 12 green

Large Heart
Cut 1 blue

Place on fold

Small Heart
Cut 10 red
Cut 10 blue

Miss Libby T. Forall

Miss Libby T. Forall
Appliqué picture 7 1/2" x 9 1/2"
Stitched by Terry Thompson
Punchneedle Picture by Susie Keply, Independence, Missouri

Miss Libby T. Forall Appliqué picture

7 1/2" x 9 1/2"
This is not for beginners.

PREPARATION

Keep all pieces in a zipper bag. The best way to appliqué Libby is in small sections at a time. Follow my step by step guide and she will go together nicely.

FABRIC REQUIREMENTS

Use scraps, but avoid plaids or any fabric that easily ravels.

- Gold for crown and belt
- Brown for hair
- Peach or tan for face, neck, chest, and arm
- Red for top bodice and upper skirt and sleeve
- Blue for lower skirt
- Off-white small calico for stripes on skirt.
- Brown for flag pole
- Light tan dot for background of flag and under flag
- Red for flag stripes and under-flag stripes and Liberty cap.
- Blue for canton
- Quiet neutral background to show the small details of the figure.
- Frame - the size of my frame's window is 7 1/2" x 9 1/2". I added 2 extra inches to wrap around the cardboard.
- Cardboard or foamcore for the backing of the picture
- Freezer paper for templates.
- Soak all scraps and press so freezer paper will easily adhere.
- Hand appliqué, or if you are brave, machine appliqué. Remember, pieces are very small.

CUTTING DIRECTIONS

- Trace each pattern on the dull side of freezer paper. Trace around templates on the right side of fabric.
- Cut out each piece and label it, adding a scant 1/4" seam allowance as you cut.

SEWING

On the small pieces, use a blind stitch with matching cotton thread. On the larger pieces and flag, use a top running stitch for interest.

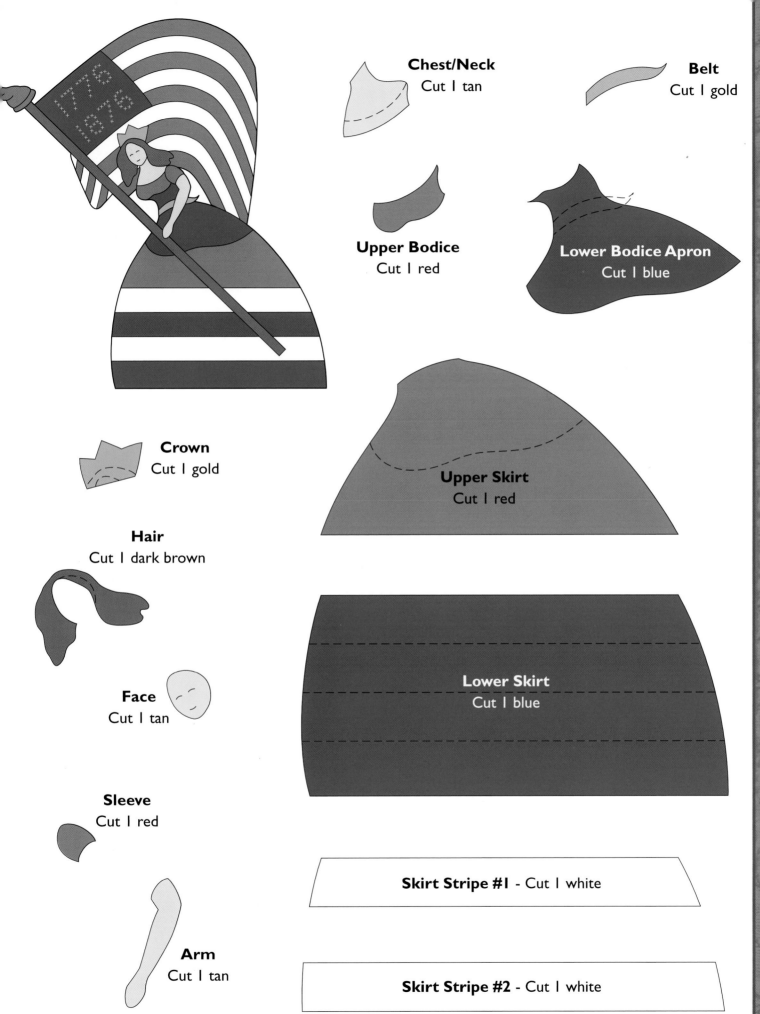

Chest/Neck
Cut 1 tan

Belt
Cut 1 gold

Upper Bodice
Cut 1 red

Lower Bodice Apron
Cut 1 blue

Crown
Cut 1 gold

Upper Skirt
Cut 1 red

Hair
Cut 1 dark brown

Face
Cut 1 tan

Lower Skirt
Cut 1 blue

Sleeve
Cut 1 red

Skirt Stripe #1 - Cut 1 white

Arm
Cut 1 tan

Skirt Stripe #2 - Cut 1 white

LIBBY

- Lay out all pieces on a flannel board in front of you.
- Begin at the top and work down.
- Sew the crown to the hair. Always refer to the drawing for placement.
- Sew the face to the hair.
- Sew the top bodice to the chest, then the chest to the face.
- Sew lower bodice, then belt.
- Sew sleeve cap over the top of the arm. Place arm and sleeve beside bodice and sew. Leave the hand unsewn until you stitch the flag pole.
- Sew the lower bodice to the upper skirt.
- Sew the white stripes to the lower skirt.

FLAG AND UNDER-FLAG

- Cut out background for the flag. This will serve as the white stripes of the flag, so all you have to sew are the red stripes onto the lines of the flag background. Baste a line of thread of the dimension of the window of your frame, so you can easily stay within the lines as you appliqué.
- Lay out the red stripes on the background and sew in place. (Remove the freezer paper and baste each piece first.
- Cut out the flag pole and Liberty cap.
- Sew the canton (Libby didn't notice the stars were missing.) Make xx's for stars or use the 1776-1876 dates to print on canton.
- Place the flag pole, and underflag at an angle across Libby's body and under her hand. Appliqué in place.
- Place the Liberty cap at top of pole.

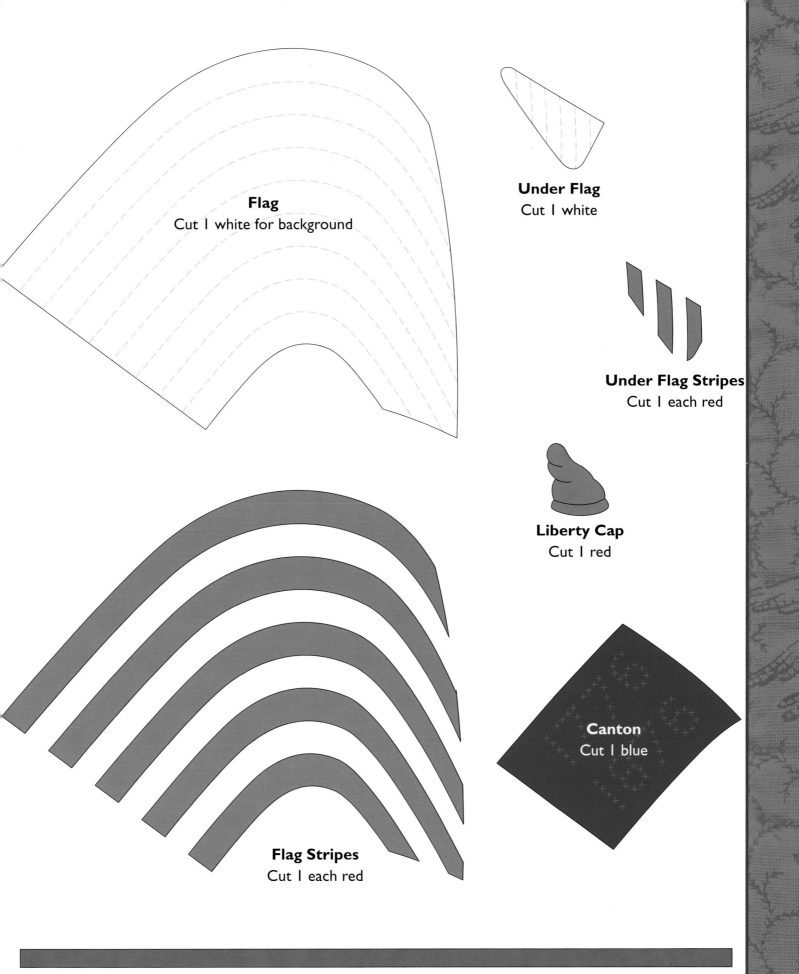

Flag
Cut 1 white for background

Under Flag
Cut 1 white

Under Flag Stripes
Cut 1 each red

Liberty Cap
Cut 1 red

Canton
Cut 1 blue

Flag Stripes
Cut 1 each red

Flag Pole
Cut 1 brown

Miss Libby T. Forall Punch Needle Picture

Punched by Susie Keply

Susie Keply punch needled this sweet miniature of Miss Liberty. Her advice is if you have never punch needled, buy a Cameo Needlepunch kit which has great instructions on how to use the needle.

As in most needlework sewn by humans, some little mistakes appear, as in the flag canton numbers. 1886 should read 1876, but I think it is charming and I am leaving it in.

SUPPLIES
Susie used embroidery floss thread in these colors:
- Tan for face, chest and arm
- Red for bodice, sleeve, flag stripes, skirt and mouth
- Gold for crown, belt, star on pole, and letters in canton. (The star at the end of the flag is partly hidden by the frame, so make sure your frame holds the entire design.)
- Blue for canton for flag, lower bodice, and the stripes in the skirt
- White for the stars in the bodice, and stripes in the flag
- Brown for hair, eyes, and the pole
- 1 - 10" square of Cameo's Candlelite poly-cotton weaver's cloth
- Frame, either old or new with at least a 4 1/2" x 5 1/2" window

- To transfer pattern, use a light box. Place pattern on box, fabric over pattern and trace with a #2 lead pencil. The pattern is punched from the back of the fabric, so pattern will be reversed. Choose the direction you want her to face.

Front

Back

Women's Sewing Pocket

Women's Sewing Pockets
Stitched by Terry Thompson

FABRIC REQUIREMENTS

- 🌸 2 yards twill tape for each pocket for ties
- 🌸 Pocket and lining - 1/2 yard print for pocket and 1/2 yard contrasting plaid or print for lining
- 🌸 Scrap of green and pink for flower stem and leaf.
- 🌸 1/2 yard bias for finishing slit and top of pocket.
- 🌸 For patchwork pocket, use a variety of sewing scraps to make 47 - 1 3/4" squares
- 🌸 1/2 yard for lining

CUTTING AND SEWING POCKET PATTERNS

- 🌸 Tape top and bottom half of pattern, lining up the fold line and outside curve of pattern.
- 🌸 Fold fabric in half and lay pattern fold line over fold line. Cut one front and one back for pocket and one front and one back for lining. Add 1/4" seam allowance as you cut.
- 🌸 For pieced pocket, cut (47) 1 3/4" squares out of sewing scraps and sew together in rows, starting at the bottom of pocket, with 8 squares, row #1. Repeat for row #2, 6 squares for rows #3, 4, 5 and 7. Row 7 & 8, 4 squares. This will give you the yardage to lay out the pattern for the pocket. Cut a lining.
- 🌸 Appliqué flower, cut a 1/2" stem, appliqué stem and leaf to front of pocket.
- 🌸 On front of pocket, cut a line 7 1/4" long down the middle of the top of the pocket - see pattern.
- 🌸 You may bind this slit or fold back the edges 2 3/4" from the art line to reveal more of the lining.
- 🌸 Sew linings for pockets.
- 🌸 With the wrong sides together, slip the lining into the pocket, pushing it to the bottom. Line up the top of the pocket and lining so that they are even.
- 🌸 Cut bias strips: 1 1/2" wide x 30" long.
- 🌸 Starting at the back of the pocket, bind the top, then down the slit and up the other side. After binding, whipstitch over the top of the pocket, front to back.

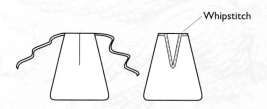

Whipstitch

- 🌸 Measure waist for length of twill tape for ties.
- 🌸 Attach twill tape to each side of the pocket.

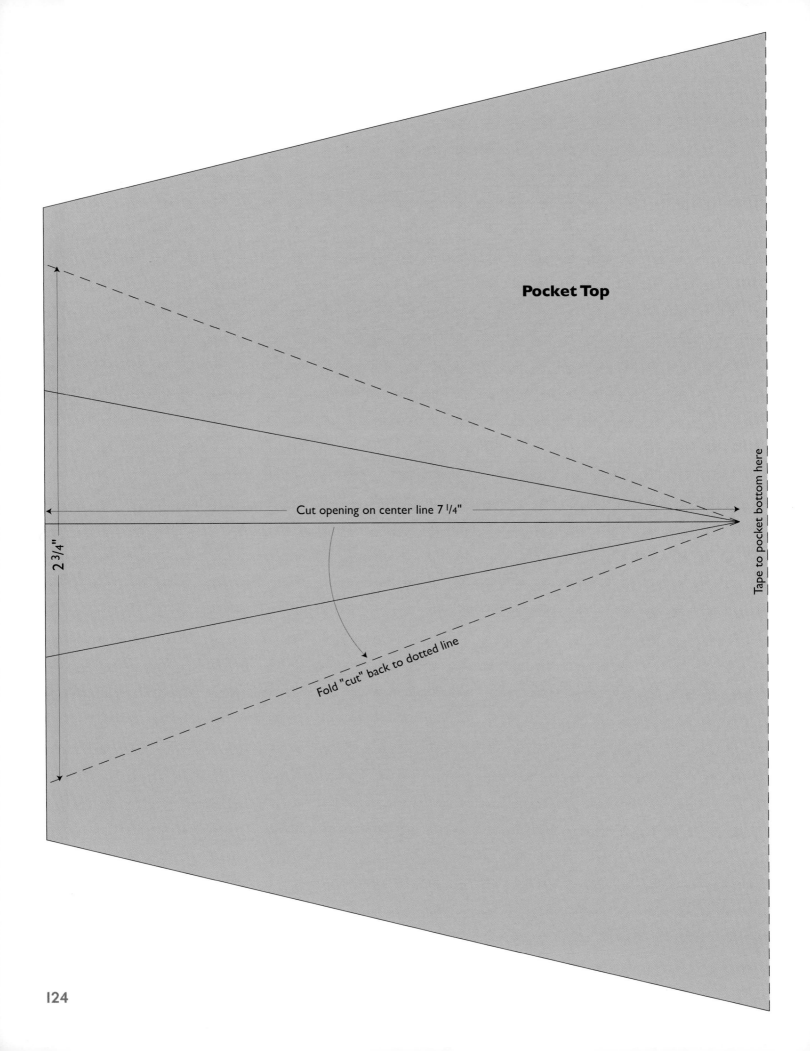

Pocket Top

2 ³/₄"

Cut opening on center line 7 ¹/₄"

Fold "cut" back to dotted line

Tape to pocket bottom here

124

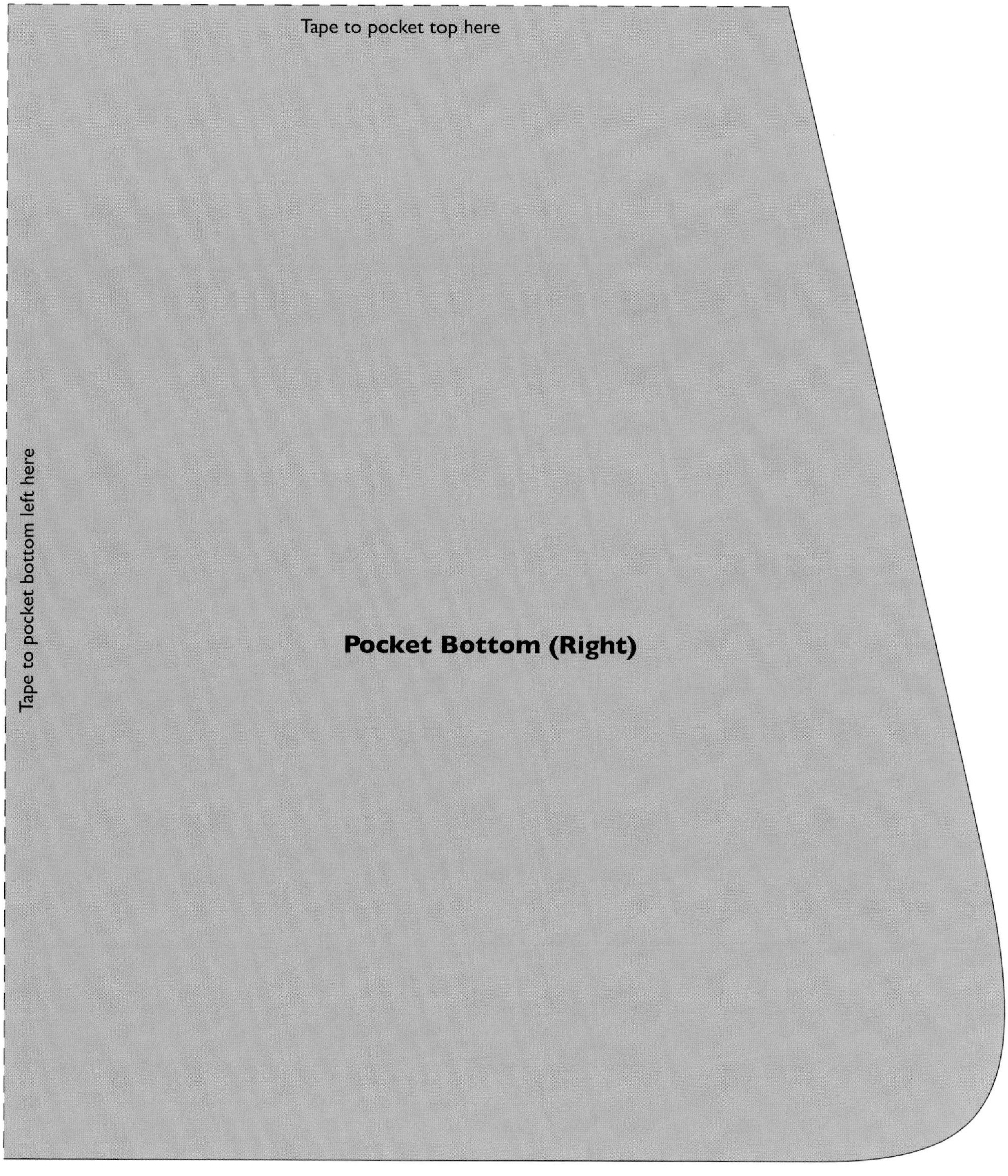

Tape to pocket top here

Tape to pocket bottom left here

Pocket Bottom (Right)

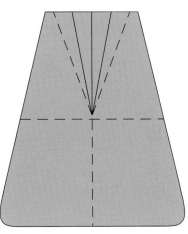

Tape together the top, bottom right and bottom left templates as shown. Cut 1 front and 1 back for pocket. Cut 1 front and one back for lining. Use contrasting fabric.

Tape to pocket top here

Pocket Bottom (Left)

Tape to pocket bottom right here

Embroidered Flag

Embroidered Flag picture
10 1/2" x 20"
Anonymous

Embroidered Flag

This vintage embroidered flag probably came as a kit with a stamped background from the 1900-1920s. I framed it in an old frame and the top and bottom borders barely fit. I covered a piece of cardboard with a red calico because the sides didn't quite fit, either. I just liked the look.

FABRIC REQUIREMENTS

❀ 20 1/2" x 10 1/2" of a black fabric that is not too tightly woven. Check craft and quilt shops that carry supplies for embroidery, fabric, and thread for counted thread crossstitch.

❀ Use #8 perle cotton or embroidery floss in red, white, and blue colors. Get at least 2 to 3 skeins of each color. Use a #7 embroidery needle.

To transfer the pattern use a transfer pen or use the method for transferring the pattern on the hooked snowflake rug. Use a light marker to trace on to the dark background.

SEWING DIRECTIONS

Outline the border design in white, using a stem stitch. Make xx's for stars.

❀ The flag, pole, tassels, and stars are worked in a long filler stitch. Stars are outlined first with a small straight stitch.

❀ Fringe edges of picture if you desire.

Join the 2 flag template
pieces together to make
full size flag template.

USA Centennial, 1876

New Centennial quilt
67 1/2" × 72 1/2"
Stitched by Jean Stanclift
Quilted by Lori Kukuk • McClouth, Kansas

USA Centennial, 1876

For the confident quilter.

FABRIC REQUIREMENTS

FOR 16 - 12" FINISHED BLOCKS AND BORDERS

- 1 yard blue for stars
- 1 yard solid red for 4-patch squares
- 1 3/4 yards red printed calico for borders
- 4 1/2 yards light tan print for blocks and borders
- 1 1/4 yards blue print for binding

ROTARY CUTTING DIRECTIONS

For 16 - 12" finished blocks, cut:

- 352 - 1 1/2" tan squares for 4-patch centers.
- 160 - 1 1/2" red squares for 4-patch centers.
- 64 - 4 1/2" tan squares.
- 64 - 1 7/8" red squares.
- 372 - 1 7/8" blue squares.
- 436 - 1 7/8" tan squares.

FOR BLUE STARS IN SASHING AND BORDERS

- 13 - 2 1/2" blue squares.
- 52 - 1 1/2" tan squares.

FOR SASHING STRIPS AND BORDERS

- 48 - 1 1/2" x 12 1/2" red strips for vertical sashing.
- 24 - 2 1/2" x 12 1/2" tan strips for vertical borders.
- 6 - 1 1/2" x 60 1/2" red strips for left, right and side borders.
- 1 - 4 1/2" x 60 1/2" red strip for top border.
- 3 - 2 1/2" x 60 1/2" tan strips for 2 sides and bottom border.
- 1 - 6 1/2" x 68 1/2" tan strip for top border.

SEWING DIRECTIONS

- Make 80 4-patch blocks for the centers of the 5 star units in each of the 16 blocks.

HOW TO MAKE HALF-INCH SQUARE TRIANGLES

- Draw a diagonal line from corner to corner on the wrong side of each tan square.

🦋 Draw a line 1/4" on either side of the diagonal line. Place a tan square atop a blue square, right sides facing, and sew on each side of the diagonal line.

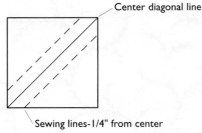

Center diagonal line

Sewing lines-1/4" from center

🦋 Cut the squares apart on the center diagonal line. Press the seam allowance toward the darker fabric.

🦋 Notice the center star of each block has 4 red and tan corner squares. Each of the 4 corner stars has 1 red and tan corner that touches the red and tan corners of the center block. Follow the half-square triangle directions above, substituting the blue squares with the red squares.

🦋 Each of the 16 blocks has 4 corner stars and 1 center star.

🦋 You need 40 blue/tan half-square triangles for the star's points for each block for a total of 640.

🦋 Each block has 8 red/tan half-square triangles for a total of 128.

🦋 Piece the blocks as you would a 9-patch block. Follow the color placement of the star units and piece the center star and the 4 corner stars. Set in rows of 3.

🦋 Set the blocks together with red/tan sashing (See instructions for sashing below).

🦋 Piece the 13 blue stars following the star instructions given above.

🦋 Refer to the directions for making half-square triangles given above.

🦋 For the 13 blue stars, you need to make 104 blue/tan half-square triangles.

🦋 For the 13 center squares of the blue stars, you need 13 – 2 1/2" blue squares.

🦋 For the corner tan squares, you need 52 – 1 1/2" tan squares.

SETTING THE BLOCKS

SASHING

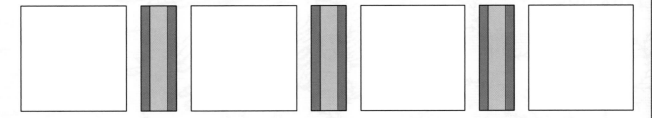

🦋 Set the 16 completed blocks in rows of 4.

🦋 Refer to page 132 for measurements.

🦋 Sew 4 rows of 4 blocks per row. You will have 4 separate rows of sashed 4-blocks.

🪶 To make the sashing, sew a red 1 1/2" x 12 1/2" strip to each side of a tan 2 1/2" x 12 1/2" strip. You will need to make 24 sashing units.

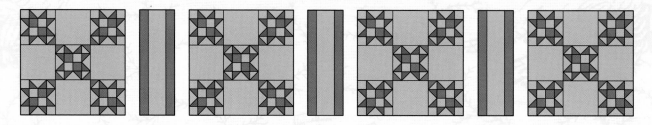

🪶 Set the blocks in rows of 4, adding the sashing between the blocks. You need 4 rows of 4.

🪶 The first and last block in each row does not need sashing on the outside edges because they will be sewn to the long side borders.

🪶 Sew a 4" blue star to the horizontal sashing at the ends of the pieced sashing units using 3 stars per row. Line up the stars in the sashing with the row above it, so each row will match. (See quilt on page 131.)

🪶 Sew a long red 4 1/2" x 60 1/2" border to the top of the quilt.

🪶 Make the bottom, right and left side borders by sewing a red 1 1/2" x 60 1/2" strip to each side of a 2 1/2" x 60 1/2" tan strip.

🪶 Place a blue star block at the top and bottom of the 2 side borders. Sew the bottom border to the quilt, then add the 2 side borders.

On the top 6 1/2" x 68 1/2" tan border embroider or appliqué the original letters "USA Centenniel 1876" or your name and year. (Notice the misspelled word "Centenniel.") I would leave this charming mistake as it is. Choose other sentiments if you wish.

🪶 Sew this border to the top of the quilt.

🪶 Quilt and bind.

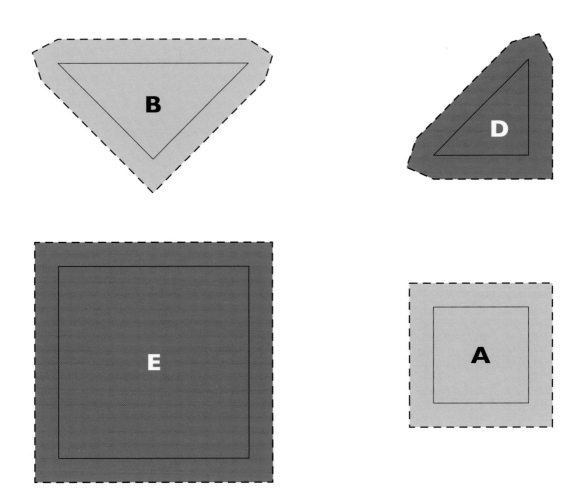

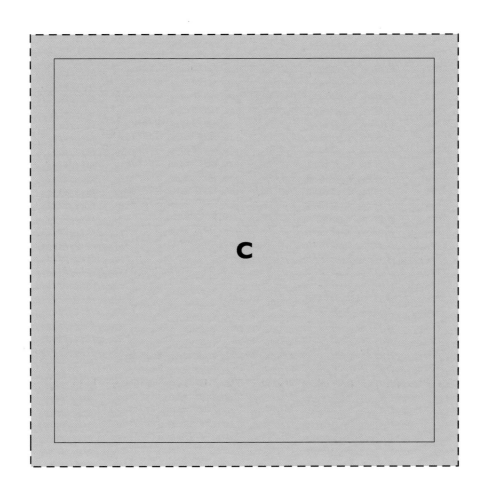

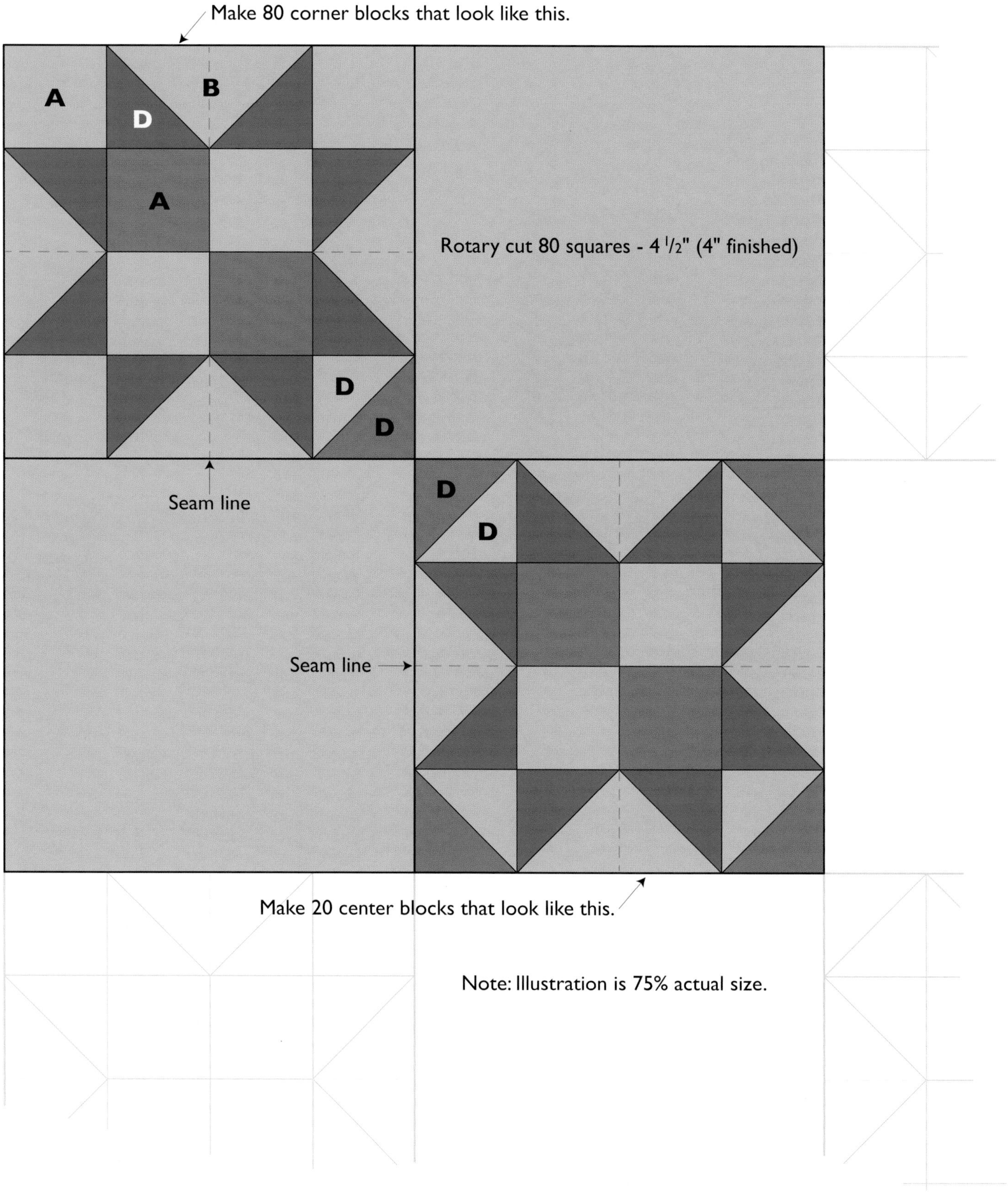

Make 80 corner blocks that look like this.

A

D

B

A

Rotary cut 80 squares - 4 ¹/₂" (4" finished)

D

D

Seam line

D

D

Seam line

Make 20 center blocks that look like this.

Note: Illustration is 75% actual size.

A B

D

E

Cut 1 1/2" x 12 1/2" (1" x 12" finished)

Cut 2 1/2" x 12 1/2" (2" x 12" finished)

Cut 1 1/2" x 12 1/2" (1" x 12" finished)

Star corner block

Horizontal connecting borders

Cut 1 1/2" x 12 1/2" (1" x 12" finished)

Cut 2 1/2" x 12 1/2" (2" x 12" finished)

Cut 1 1/2" x 12 1/2" (1" x 12" finished)

Vertical connecting borders

B

D

Note: Illustration is 50% actual size.

1876

Centennial

U.S.A.

U.S.A. Centennial 1876
"Cluster of Stars"
 68 1/2" x 72 1/2"

This vintage quilt was loaned to Terry by Leslie Snodgrass of Wichita, Kansas. It inspired the new Centennial quilt.

Leslie bought it from a quilt dealer who knew nothing of its provenance. The original colors are blue, now turned a greenish blue, and a turkey-red, which has retained its vibrant red color, and a white, now ecru, print.

The embroidered "USA Centenniel 1876" leaves no doubt that the maker sewed her own Centennial quilt. Note the charming misspelling of the name "Centenniel." Whether our unknown quilter showed this quilt at the Centennial Exhibition is not known, but it is an important, historical relic of the Centennial years and I am grateful to the 19th century quiltmaker who documented a time in American history, otherwise the quilt would be just another "Cluster of Stars."

Gallery

Nancy Wakefield
Platte City, Missouri

Judy Collins, quilt on right
Linda Kittle, quilt on left
Leavenworth, Kansas

Amanda Harker
Kansas City, Missouri

Patty Holley
Leavenworth, Kansas
Modeled by Dan, Mahaffie Historic Site, Olathe, Kansas

Anne Rielly
Leavenworth, Kansas

Linda Harker
Kansas City, Missouri

Pat Moore
Kansas City, Kansas
Alexis Radil presents a Libertyville quilt on the steps of the
Mahaffie ice house

Suzannah Christenson
Lawrence, Kansas

144

Cindy Farrell with help from Nancy Solsberg, Lora Robbins, Gayle LeMaster,
Sharon Ward and Carolyn Cargyle

from Rustic Yearnings quilt shop, Independence, Missouri

Mahaffie Stagecoach Stop and Historic Site
Olathe, Kansas

We owe our gratitude to the gracious staff at the Mahaffie Farm Historic Site who made shooting pictures for this book such a pleasure. Tim Talbott and Dewayne Hill brought out the stagecoach for us. Geoff Bahr managed Dan, the palomino. Special thanks go to Alexis Radil who provided valuable assistance, helped us show off the quilts and modeled period dress for the photos

The stone farmhouse built by James B. and Lucinda Mahaffie in 1865 is one of the few stagecoach stops left on the Santa Fe Trail, and the only one preserved as a public historic site. Along with the farmhouse, the stone ice house - also built in 1865 - and the original timber-frame barn (probably the oldest building on the site and built around 1860) are all listed on the National and Kansas Registers of Historic Places. Mahaffie is also a certified site of the Santa Fe National Historic Trail by the National Park Service.

About twenty acres remain of the original 570 acre farm, located on the "Westport Route," which actually carried traffic of all the trails leading out of Westport, Missouri: the Santa Fe, Oregon, and California Trails. The Mahaffies came to Olathe from Indiana in 1857, and purchased this farm site in 1858. They used oxen to move a portion of the wood frame home from their downtown lot to their new holdings - at that time, about a mile outside of town. The family lived in that home until the new house was built in 1865.

The Barlow and Sanderson stagecoach line contracted with the Mahaffie family to provide one of the stops needed for their coaches operating in Kansas, and carrying

passengers and the U.S. Mail from Missouri all the way to Santa Fe. From 1865 to 1869, hungry passengers took their meals in the basement of the stone farmhouse, built to serve as a kitchen and dining hall. At peak times, Lucinda, her daughters, and hired helpers may have served as many as 50 to 100 meals a day. While the passengers ate, the incoming teams of horses were switched for fresh animals. Other travelers made use of the Mahaffie home as well.

The Mahaffie home and adjoining property was purchased by the city of Olathe in 1979 to operate as a historic site, and to insure its preservation.

147

Other Star books

Star Quilts I: *One Piece at a Time* by *Kansas City Star* Books - 1999.

Star Quilts II: *More Kansas City Star Quilts* by Edie McGinnis - 2000

Star Quilts III: *Outside the Box: Hexagon Patterns from The Kansas City Star* by Edie McGinnis - 2001.

Star Quilts IV: *Prairie Flower: A Year on the Plains* by Barbara Brackman - 2001.

Star Quilts V: *The Sister Blocks* by Edie McGinnis - 2001.

Star Quilts VI: *Kansas City Quiltmakers* by Doug Worgul - 2001.

Star Quilts VII: *O'Glory: Americana Quilt Blocks from The Kansas City Star* by Edie McGinnis - 2001.

Star Quilts VIII: *Hearts & Flowers: Hand Applique From Start to Finish* by Kathy Delany - 2002.

Star Quilts IX: *Roads & Curves Ahead* by Edie McGinnis - 2002.

Star Quilts X: *Celebration of American Life: Applique Patterns Honoring a Nation and Its People* by Barb Adams and Alma Allen - 2002.

Star Quilts XI: *Women of Grace & Charm: A Quilting Tribute to the Women Who Served in World War II* by Barb Adams and Alma Allen - 2003.

Star Quilts XII: *A Heartland Album: More Techniques in Hand Appliqué* by Kathy Delany - 2003.

Star Quilts XIII: *Quilting a Poem: Designs Inspired by America's Poets* by Frances Kit and Debra Rowden - 2003.

Star Quilts XIV: *Carolyn's Paper-Pieced Garden: Patterns for Miniature and Full-Sized Quilts* by Carolyn Cullinan McCormack - 2003.

Star Quilts XV: *Murders On Elderberry Road, a mystery book* by Sally Goldenbaum - 2003.

Star Quilts XVI: *Friendships in Bloom: Round Robin Quilts* by Marjorie Nelson & Rebecca Nelson-Zerfas - 2003.

Star Quilts XVII: *Baskets of Treasures: Designs Inspired by Life Along the River* by Edie McGinnis - 2003.

Star Quilts XVIII: *Heart & Home: Unique American Women and the Houses that Inspire* by Kathy Schmitz - 2003.

Star Quilts XIX: *Women of Design: Quilts in the Newspaper* by Barbara Brackman - 2004.

Star Quilts XX: *The Basics: An Easy Guide to Beginning Quiltmaking* by Kathy Delaney - 2004.

Star Quilts XXI: *Four Block Quilts: Echoes of History, Pieced Boldly & Appliquéd Freely* by Terry Clothier Thompson - 2004.

Star Quilts XXII: *No Boundaries: Bringing Your Fabric Over The Edge* by Edie McGinnis - 2004.

Star Quilts XXIII: *Horn of Plenty for a New Century* by Kathy Delaney - 2004.

Star Quilts XXIV: *Quilting the Garden* by Barb Adams and Alma Allen - 2004.

Star Quilts XXV: *A Murder of Taste: A Queen Bee Quilt Mystery* by Sally Goldenbaum - 2004

Star Quilts XXVI: *Patterns of History: Moda Fabric Challenge* by Barbara Brackman - 2004.

Star Quilts XXVII: *Stars All Around Us: Quilts and Projects Inspired by a Beloved Symbol* by Cherie Ralston - 2005.

Star Quilts XXVIII: *Quilters' Stories: Collecting History in the Heart of America* by Debra Rowden - 2005.

Star Quilts XXIX: *Libertyville, Where Liberty Dwells, There is My Country,* by Terry Clothier Thompson - 2005.

Star Quilts XXX: *Sparkling Jewels, Pearls of Wisdom* by Edie McGinnis - 2005.

Star Quilts XXXI: *Grapefruit Juice and Sugar* by Jenifer Dick - 2005.

Star Quilts XXXII: *Home Sweet Home* by Barb Adams and Alma Allen - 2005.

Star Quilts XXXIII: *Patterns of History: The Challenge Winners - 23 Quilt Designs Inspired by Our Past* by Kathy Delaney - 2005.

PROJECT BOOKS:

Santa's Parade of Nursery Rhymes by Jeanne Poore - 2000.

Fan Quilt Memories: A Selection of Fan Quilts from The Kansas City Star by Jeanne Poore - 2001.

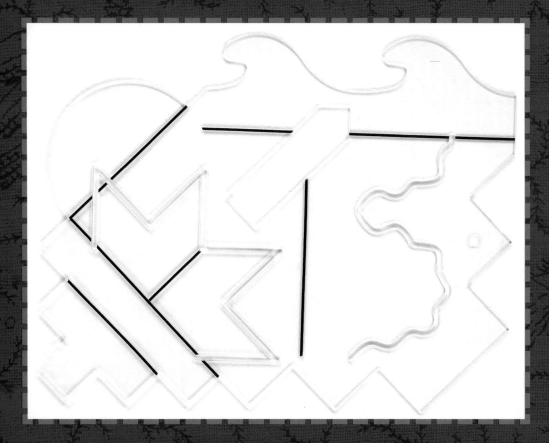

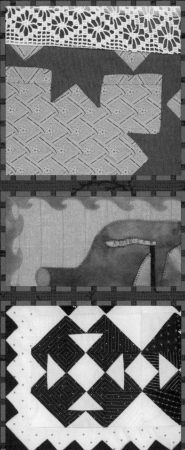

The Original Border Line
For Borders and Corners
Designed by Terry Clothier Thompson

Terry Clothier Thompson, creator of *The Original Vine Line*, has come up with a NEW tool for marking borders and corners. **The Border Line** has seven unique appliquéd border shapes using traditional designs taken from vintage quilts. The tool is perfect for wool penny mats and hooked rugs, as well as quilts. And because it's always an issue, Terry solved the problem of making the corners come out even.

Detailed illustrations and directions for using **The Border Line**, plus all the applique' patterns shown on the cover, are included in the package.

Here are the Designs: **Picket Fence** used in 1920's -30's quilts, the **Star**, **Stair Steps** and **Dogtooth** from c. 1848 - 1875 quilts; **Wave** and **Half Circle** from vintage rugs and penny mats; the **Tidewater** border from 1780's - 90's quilts from Maryland and Virginia. Tool measures 8 1/2" x 11".

All of these designs are packed into one amazingly versatile tool. Made of impact resistant PETG plastic, **The Original Border Line** is one tool no quilter should be without. (The other is *The Original Vine Line*.) Do yourself a favor, and get a tool that will be used time and time again, for all of your quilting projects - **The Original Border Line**.

You can purchase the **Original Border Line** for $24 at your local quilt or fabric store, or order directly through Kansas City Star Quilt's on-line store. Go to www.PickleDish.com. Or call us toll-free at 1-866-834-7467.